Software Reuse

Guidelines and Methods

Software Science and Engineering

Series Editor: **Richard A. DeMillo**
Purdue University, West Lafayette, Indiana

High-Integrity Software
Edited by C. T. Sennett

Software Reuse: Guidelines and Methods
James W. Hooper and Rowena O. Chester

A Continuation Order Plan is available for this series. A continuation order will bring delivery of each new volume immediately upon publication. Volumes are billed only upon actual shipment. For further information please contact the publisher.

Software Reuse

Guidelines and Methods

James W. Hooper
The University of Alabama in Huntsville
Huntsville, Alabama

and

Rowena O. Chester
Martin Marietta Energy Systems
Oak Ridge, Tennessee

Plenum Press • New York and London

Library of Congress Cataloging-in-Publication Data

Hooper, James W.
    Software reuse : guidelines and methods / James W. Hooper and
Rowena O. Chester.
        p.   cm. -- (Software science and engineering)
    Includes bibliographical references and index.
    ISBN 0-306-43918-2
    1. Computer software--Reusability.   I. Chester, R. O.   II. Title.
III. Series.
QA76.76.R47H66   1991
005--dc20   91-12080
                                                                CIP

ISBN 0-306-43918-2

© 1991 Plenum Press, New York
A Division of Plenum Publishing Corporation
233 Spring Street, New York, N.Y. 10013

Printed in the United States of America

Foreword

Observers in the present usually have an advantage when it comes to interpreting events of the past. In the case of software reuse, however, it is unclear why an idea that has gained such universal acceptance was the source of swirling controversy when it began to be taken seriously by the software engineering community in the mid-1980's.

From a purely conceptual point of view, the reuse of software designs and components promises nearly risk-free benefits to the developer. Virtually every model of software cost and development effort predicts first-order dependencies on either products size or the number of steps carried out in development. Reduce the amount of new product to be developed and the cost of producing the product decreases. Remove development steps, and total effort is reduced. By reusing previously developed engineering products the amount of new product and the number of development steps can be reduced. In this way, reuse clearly has a major influence on reducing total development cost and effort. This, of course, raises the issue of from whence the reused products arise. There has to be a prior investment in creating "libraries of reuse products before reuse can be successful..." How can organizations with a "bottom line" orientation be enticed into contributing to a reuse venture? Fortunately, the economics of reuse resembles many other financial investment situations[1]. The relevant index is the ratio $Q = \frac{B}{R}$, where, for a total reuse investment R, B is the resulting cost-benefit, i.e., the difference between the cost of the activity without reuse and the cost of the activity with the reuse investment. As Q decreases, the reuse investment becomes more advantageous. If, on the other hand, Q is greater than 1, the benefits of reuse do not justify the investment.

Furthermore, reuse also has quality implications. Reused components have, by definition, an operational history that can be used to predict their future behavior. This is itself a kind of reuse by exploiting the experience with reuse library elements, new developers can make more informed risk assessments for a new project.

---

[1] Barnes, B. and T. Bollinger. 1991. "Making Reuse Cost-Effective." *IEEE Software,* 8(1), 13–24.

None of these ideas were born in a vacuum. By the early 1970's there had already been highly successful software enterprises based on reuse. Important lessons were learned and some models were suggested for new enterprises. The most celebrated example along these lines was the growth of mathematical libraries.

These are, in fact, the very aspects of reuse that have contributed to its success as a software engineering principle. Developers, arguing from first principles, apparently could construct a compelling case that software reuse should be a cornerstone of standard practice. Controversies arose, not over the concept, but rather over its applicability in realistic environments.

Take, for example, the potential cost savings in a reuse environment. The argument that reuse reduces overall costs is based on the assumption that retrieving and reusing components or designs from a library is less expensive than recreating them. If all the costs of reuse were associated with archival characteristics, there would certainly be no disagreement over the benefits of reuse. But there are other costs that creep into the picture – interface costs, for example. If N reuse modules with average size M have to interoperate with pairwise distinct interfaces, on the order of $\binom{N}{2}$ interface might be required. The total cost of constructing these interfaces could easily outstrip the cost of constructing a program of size $N \cdot M$ without reuse.

The quality of reusable components is, of course, a significant risk factor. How does a developer know when a reused component has acceptable reliability, suddenly makes unsafe an otherwise safe system, or degrades system performance? Where is the quality history of a component stored? Do tests of components in reuse libraries have to be reexecuted?

The very question of what constitutes a library of reusable software component is not easy to answer. Examples of successful reuse such as math libraries are not as easy to generalize as it might seem. Mathematical software happens to be a field in which the appropriate "chunk size" is given by the application: a function that implements a standard numerical algorithm is exactly the right size. But there are areas in which there are not convenient chunks. What is the appropriate component in such an environment? Perhaps more importantly: can a library be constructed that facilitates user access to needed components?

Even the investment aspects of reuse present problems to software engineering projects. Software development are characterized their susceptibility to schedule and budget pressures, and the sociological processes that would lead a manager with short-term objectives to

make a long-term investment in reuse were not defined to any useful
degree.

The US Army Institute for Research in Management Information,
Communications, and Computer Sciences (AIRMICS) had recognized
that effective programs for reuse and the supporting technology would
be difficult to develop without principles, "lessons-learned", and case
studies to guide managers and engineers. AIRMICS initiated and supported the study that led to the present volume. When the history of
software engineering in the 1980's is written, this study will be recognized as a pivotal event in the birth of one of the key generalizations
of software engineering – one of the concepts that helped turn it from
a cottage industry to an engineering technology.

Richard A. DeMillo
Washington, DC

February 1991

Preface

Software reuse is currently receiving a great deal of attention. This interest is fueled by the urgent need for greater software productivity and quality, coupled with the growing belief that software reuse may be able to help with these problems. Conferences and workshops on software engineering or the Ada language are almost certain to have some papers on reuse—and perhaps multiple sessions devoted to the topic. Refereed software engineering journals are publishing many articles on reuse as well.

This book attempts to achieve two related goals:

(a) providing a cogent summary of current research and practice in software reuse, and

(b) providing practical suggestions for integrating software reuse into a software engineering process.

The first goal is important because the body of literature is now very large, and the field is so broad that it is difficult to gain a good grasp of the issues. We have developed a framework for presenting the material that should help the reader achieve a perspective of the field. We have condensed a great deal of material covering both research and practice. Some of it is useful now, while some of it provides insights into issues whose solution will permit future gains from reuse. Even though some incompletely resolved issues remain, we believe that benefits can be gained now from software reuse—thus leading to the second goal stated above. This book includes guidelines for integrating reuse into a software engineering process and for conducting reuse activities. We sought to propose guidelines that are not dogmatic, but rather suggestive of important activities and approaches. The guidelines may alternatively be viewed as summarizing current knowledge about reuse practice. The level of detail of the guidelines varies depending on how well the issues are currently understood. We hope they will be helpful as presented and that in time each organization that undertakes reuse will evolve its own set of tailored guidelines.

Various audiences should find this book useful. Software engineering managers and practitioners should benefit from the guidelines, with their supporting rationale, and from descriptions of successful reuse projects. The presentation of research and practice material in an intelligible framework, augmented by the extensive bibliography, should be useful to computer science and software engineering educators and students as well as researchers in universities, government, and industry. Multiple approaches and viewpoints are discussed for many reuse issues to provide a basis for further experimentation and research. Discussions of specific research and practice findings are accompanied by references to the literature; thus the book contains in essence an extensive annotated bibliography, which can be a valuable resource to researchers.

We developed and issued much of this material under the Ada Reuse and Metrics Project (Hooper and Chester 1990), conducted by Martin Marietta Energy Systems under contract to the U.S. Army Institute for Research in Management Information, Communications, and Computer Sciences (AIRMICS). We express our appreciation to Dan Hocking, who served as the project manager for that work at AIRMICS. His insightful comments and suggestions led to the development of more useful results than would otherwise have been the case, and this book has in turn benefitted. Funding for the AIRMICS Ada Reuse and Metrics Project was provided by the U.S. Department of Defense (DOD) Software Technology for Adaptable, Reliable Systems (STARS) program. Other technical contributors to the Ada Reuse and Metrics Project included Victor R. Basili (University of Maryland, College Park); Terry B. Bollinger (CONTEL); Richard A. DeMillo (Purdue University); Richard E. Fairley (George Mason University); Ross A. Gagliano (Georgia State University); Arthur Jones (Morehouse College); Roger King (University of Colorado at Boulder); Rhonda Martin (Purdue University); W. Michael McCracken (Georgia Institute of Technology); Charles W. McKay (University of Houston, Clear Lake); Shari Lawrence Pfleeger (CONTEL); and H. Dieter Rombach (University of Maryland, College Park).

We express our appreciation to James Baldo and Ruben Prieto-Diaz for reviewing and commenting on the manuscript. A number of improvements resulted from their suggestions. We also thank Patricia Mucke for her invaluable editorial assistance and Ramez Abi Akar for his careful reading of the manuscript.

James W. Hooper
Huntsville, Alabama

Rowena O. Chester
Oak Ridge, Tennessee

February 1991

Contents

3. Technical Guidelines

4. Getting Started

Acronyms

4GL	Fourth-generation language
AdaIC	Ada Information Clearinghouse
AFATDS	U.S. Army Advanced Field Artillery Tactical Data System
AIRMICS	U.S. Army Institute for Research in Management Information, Communications, and Computer Sciences
AJPO	DOD Ada Joint Program Office
ALS	Automated Library System
ARSC	Applications of Reusable Software Components
ASGS	Automatic Software Generation System
BNF	Backus-Naur Form
CAMP	Common Ada Missile Packages
CASE	Computer-aided software engineering tools
CECOM	U.S. Army Communications Electronics Command
CSD	Cost sharing domain
DOD	U.S. Department of Defense
EAP	Experimental Aircraft Programme in the United Kingdom
EI	Extension Interpreter
ER	Entity-relationship
ERA	Entity-relationship-attribute
ESF	European Software Factory
ESL	Entity Specification Language
FFP	Firm fixed price
GSFC	NASA Goddard Space Flight Center
IDeA	Intelligent Design Aid
IR	Information retrieval
ISEC	U.S. Army Information Systems Engineering Command
JIAWG	DOD Joint Integrated Avionics Working Group
LIL	Library Interconnection Language
NASA	National Aeronautics and Space Administration
NRL	Naval Research Laboratory
OOD	Object-oriented design

OPTI	Department of Commerce Office of Productivity, Technology, and Innovation
PDL	Program design language
PROTO	Tool for functional prototyping
RADC	U.S. Air Force Rome Air Development Center
RAPID	Reusable Ada Packages for Information System Development
RCL	RAPID Center Library
REUSE	Westinghouse Reusability Search Expert
REX	Resource Extractor
RSL	Reusable Software Library
SADT	Systems Analysis and Design Technique
SDC	U.S. Army Strategic Defense Command
SEI	Software Engineering Institute
SPC	Software Productivity Consortium
SPS	Software Productivity Solutions, Inc.
SQL	Structured Query Language
SRE	Software Reuse Environment
STARS	Software Technology for Adaptable, Reliable Systems
V&V	Validation and verification
VLSR	Very large scale reuse

Background and Introduction

1.1 The Problem

Even though expenditures for software are escalating, productivity is falling behind the demand for new software. Delivered software is often of poor quality and very difficult (and expensive) to maintain. The same trends are perceivable throughout the software industry. Software reuse, however, has the potential to increase productivity, reduce costs, and improve software quality. Jones (1984) estimates that of all the code written in 1983, probably less than 15 percent was unique, novel, and specific to individual applications. Thus an obvious candidate area for increasing productivity and reducing cost is to reuse existing software products to achieve all or part of the redundant 85 percent of the development. An estimated average of only about 5 percent of code is actually reused (Frakes and Nejmeh 1987, quoting DeMarco). Software quality improvements are expected to come from the greater use and testing of individual components, with the resulting isolation and correction of any problems discovered.

Wegner (1984) notes that the importance of software libraries of reusable programs was recognized by Wilkes, Wheeler, and Gill as early as 1950. Wegner also notes that in 1969 McdIlroy proposed a reusable software components technology to parallel components technologies for products such as automobiles. Wegner quotes McIlroy as follows:

> I would like to see the study of software components become a dignified branch of software engineering. I would like to see standard catalogs of routines classified by precision, robustness, time-space requirements and binding time of parameters.

Some software reuse has occurred for many years, of course, beginning with libraries of mathematical subroutines and now including libraries of operating systems, language processors, report generators, compiler generators, fourth-generation languages, and many application-specific packages. To achieve the needed benefits, however, software reuse must be expanded much further—to "reuse in the large"—to cope with the size and complexity of current software.

Software reuse cannot be successful in isolation; it must be applied within a framework of effective software engineering practice including organizational structure, life-cycle process (policies, methods, tools, etc.), and well-trained personnel.

1.2 Concepts and Definitions

The candidate products for reuse may be considered and characterized relative to activities of the software development and maintenance process. We can characterize these activities as:

- domain analysis
- requirements specification
- high-level design
- detailed design
- coding and unit testing
- integration testing
- documentation
- maintenance

In principle, we expect greater returns from the reuse of the products of higher-level abstraction activities. Thus, a reused requirements specification gives us greater leverage than a reused code module. Only part of the knowledge gained from the software life-cycle activities is recorded and retained. In addition to requirements specifications, designs, code, test documents, test cases, integration plan, etc., lessons learned about the application domain during a project and rationale for design decisions, tradeoff considerations in decomposition and allocation to system components, etc., should be recorded. Almost always some knowledge is factored out through the refinement process; but knowledge acquired during a project is exceedingly valuable for retention.

Since experienced personnel naturally retain much knowledge of their previous work, reuse of personnel is extremely advantageous in software development within an application area. Also, reuse of the software development/maintenance process(es) used within an organization can be a great advantage. Personnel learn how to approach problem solutions in a systematic way, and they benefit from the repetitive application of the process. Tracz (1990) divides software reuse into three areas: product, process, and personnel. He points out that these could also be called, in order, what, when, and who.

Basili et al. (1987) list the same three kinds of potential reuse as Tracz does (personnel, process, and products), and further characterize them as the reuse of knowledge that exists only within the minds of people (informal knowledge), reuse of specified plans on how to perform certain activities or structure and document certain products (schematized knowledge), and reuse of tools and products (productized knowledge). Basili et al. also note that successes in software reuse are due to the characteristics of reused components, the characteristics of the reuse process, and the environment in which reuse takes place.

In this book, the term software component (or component) is used to mean any type of software resource that may be reused (e.g., code modules, designs, requirements specifications, domain knowledge, development experience, or documentation).

The way we define terms is critical, since our understanding is determined (focused or limited) by our definitions. Two possible definitions of software reusability are:

1. the extent to which a software component can be used (with or without adaptation) in multiple problem solutions;
2. the extent to which a software component can be used (with or without adaptation) in a problem solution other than the one for which it was originally developed.

Definition 2 suggests that reusability is an incidental result from software development; definition 1 suggests planned efforts toward reusability. While the prefix "re" of the word reusability may inherently suggest definition 2, definition 1 appears to be a more productive and better-focused definition and better characterizes current thinking. Perhaps definition 2 better characterizes previous achievements, and definition 1 recognizes the need to emphasize reusability as a worthy focus within itself.

Clearly, software reuse is the goal, while software reusability is necessary in order to achieve the goal. Tracz's view of software reuse (Tracz 1990) is consistent with definition 1 for software reusability; he views it as the process of reusing software that was designed to be reused, which is distinct from reusing software that was not designed for reuse (software salvaging) and from carrying over code from one version of an application to another. The following definitions of reuse are consistent with definition 1:

- Reuse is an act of synthesizing a solution to a problem based on predefined solutions to subproblems (Kang 1987).
- Reuse is the process of implementing new software systems from pre-existing software (AdaIC, 1990, quoting Cohen).
- Reuse is the reapplication of a variety of kinds of knowledge about one system to another similar system in order to re-

duce the effort of development and maintenance of that other
system (Biggerstaff and Perlis 1989a).

- Reuse is the process by which existing software work products
(which may include not only source code, but also products
such as documentation, designs, test data, tools, and specifications) are carried over and used in a new development effort,
preferably with minimal modification (Bollinger and Pfleeger
1990).

Biggerstaff and Perlis make it clear in their discussion that they do
not expect such reuse to occur incidentally—it must be planned for
and capitalized. Section 2.1.4 discusses their comments in detail.

There are numerous implications of software reuse, including recognizing the desirability of retaining certain predefined solutions for
reuse; codifying and retaining the solutions (i.e., components); recognizing the availability of potentially applicable components during
solution of a problem; and adapting and composing the components
into software that provides a valid problem solution. To achieve software reuse, means must be provided to deal with these implications.
The focus of this book is to consider various means devised to deal
with the issues and to offer guidelines for instituting software reuse
within an organization.

Portability is a characteristic of software closely related to
reusability. Portability refers to the extent to which a software component can be used in multiple machine environments (the physical hardware, operating system, run-time environment, and compiler
conventions). Thus reusability includes portability in the sense that
portability is necessary to achieve reusability across multiple machine
environments. Section 3.2.4, Component Quality, considers the interrelationships between portability and adaptability.

1.3 Research Activities

Both in the U.S. and abroad (especially in Europe and Japan) a
great deal of research is underway to achieve effective software reuse.
Although it is not our purpose to present detailed coverage of ongoing
research projects, it is useful to present an indication of the extent
of reuse research activity as a measure of the importance currently
placed on software reuse.

The Common Ada Missile Packages (CAMP) project (Anderson
and McNicholl 1985; McNicholl et al. 1986), conducted by McDonnell Douglas under contract to the U.S. Department of Defense (DOD)
Software Technology for Adaptable, Reliable Systems (STARS) program, has proven to be one of the most important reuse research

projects conducted. The federally funded Software Engineering Institute (SEI) at Carnegie-Mellon University in Pittsburgh conducted the Applications of Reusable Software Components (ARSC) project, experimenting with the CAMP reusable parts (Holibaugh 1989). The Domain Analysis project is now underway at SEI (summarized in section 3.1.2). The work emphasizes various facets of reuse, including domain analysis and domain-specific software architectures. The U.S. Army Communications Electronics Command (CECOM) Center for Software Engineering also is conducting research based on the CAMP parts. STARS efforts also resulted in the development of a reusability guidebook (Wald 1986), and STARS is now undertaking a major reuse research project involving support from Boeing, IBM, and Unisys.

U.S. Army Institute for Research in Management Information, Communications, and Computer Sciences (AIRMICS) has sponsored reuse research at a number of universities and institutions (Hooper and Chester 1990). Martin Marietta Energy Systems directed the research, and the STARS program was the funding source. The Reusable Ada Packages for Information System Development (RAPID) Center project is being conducted by SofTech for the U.S. Army Information Systems Engineering Command (ISEC); it emphasizes the identification and retrieval of reusable Ada software components (Guerrieri 1988; Vogelsong 1989). ISEC also sponsored SofTech's work in preparing guidelines for reuse (ISEC 1985). SofTech also prepared guidelines for the U.S. Air Force Electronic Systems Division (Braun, Goodenough, and Eaves 1985). Honeywell prepared guidelines for reusable Ada code under funding from the Office of Naval Research (St. Dennis 1986). U.S. Air Force Rome Air Development Center (RADC) has sponsored reuse research (Presson et al. 1983).

The Software Productivity Consortium (SPC) in Reston, Virginia, conducts reuse research, including studies involving cost modeling for reuse assessment and relationships between reuse and prototyping (Pyster and Barnes 1987; Barnes et al. 1987a, 1987b). The Microelectronics and Computer Technology Corporation (MCC) in Austin, Texas, is conducting research in many facets of reuse, including the application of reverse engineering methods and hypermedia to reuse, and reuse of software components across the life cycle, which is called wide-spectrum reuse (Biggerstaff and Richter 1987; Biggerstaff 1989; Lubars 1987).

Numerous companies are active in reuse research and experimentation. In addition to those already mentioned, some others are: Computer Sciences Corporation, Computer Technology Associates, CONTEL Technology Center, Draper Labs, GTE, Institute for Defense Analyses, Rational, SAIC, and Westinghouse. A summary of some reuse projects as of 1987 may be found in Tracz 1988a.

Significant research projects are underway in the United Kingdom, as evidenced by the special section on software reuse in the September 1988 issue of the Software Engineering Journal (Hall 1988); this issue contains some excellent research papers. The European Software Factory (ESF) is a multination project to advance reuse knowledge/practice in Europe. A recent paper on the Japanese "software factory" approach is Fujino 1987.

Many conferences and workshops dealing with software reuse are being held, and refereed journal articles on reuse are becoming more numerous. The nature of the papers shows that research issues are becoming more focused, and progress is evident. This book's bibliography includes many papers on research results. A seminal reference is the landmark September 1984 issue on software reusability of the *IEEE Transactions on Software Engineering* (Biggerstaff and Perlis 1984). Another important source is the July 1987 special issue of *IEEE Software*, "Making Reuse a Reality" (Tracz 1987a). An outstanding paper is Biggerstaff and Richter 1987. Three tutorials are available: Freeman 1987, Tracz 1988b, and Biggerstaff and Perlis 1989a and 1989b.

1.4 Status of Reuse Practice

Reuse concepts are moving from research into practice, and very good results are being reported. An initial investment in reuse (organizational changes, initial library development, training, etc.) is required, and there has been an understandable reluctance to make this investment without reasonable assurance of success. Enough reuse successes are accumulating to allay the concerns; thus we expect an increase in the number of organizations undertaking the practice of software reuse. A number of the successes have been based on ad hoc approaches, which means that technical breakthroughs are not necessary to achieve success in software reuse, although productivity can certainly be further improved. We consider in this section a number of successful reuse projects as well as some mechanisms now available to support reuse.

The DOD Ada Software Repository and AdaNET are reuse support mechanisms now in place. The DOD Ada Software Repository was established in 1984 to promote the exchange and use of public-domain Ada programs and tools, and to promote Ada education by providing several working examples of programs in source code form to study and to modify. The repository contains source code exceeding 20 MB in size. Conn (1986) provides an overview of the

DOD Ada Software Repository and explains how to obtain access to available services. AdaNET is a government-sponsored information service, established in October 1988 to facilitate the transfer of federally developed software engineering and Ada technology to the private sector. It is operated by MountainNet, Inc., Dellslow, West Virginia, and sponsored by the National Aeronautics and Space Administration (NASA) Technology Utilization Division, DOD Ada Joint Program Office (AJPO), and Department of Commerce Office of Productivity, Technology, and Innovation (OPTI). AdaNET offers 24-hour on-line computer access to information about Ada software, bibliographies, conferences and seminars, education and training, news events, products, reference materials, and standards. Interested organizations and individuals are invited to call MountainNet for detailed information, including how to apply for an AdaNET Electronic Mail Account. (The telephone number is 304-296-1458.) Both of these software reuse support mechanisms, the Ada Software Repository and AdaNET, have the potential to provide practical help to organizations practicing reuse, although their use to date has been limited. Since these organizations were established at an early point in the development of software reuse methods and practices, prospective users should carefully examine available components relative to current software engineering guidelines in their organization.

A number of documents are available that offer guidance in software reuse—primarily in preparing Ada code for reuse. These include ISEC 1985; Braun, Goodenough, and Eaves 1985; Wald 1986; and St. Dennis 1986. This book has drawn from these guides and covers a wider range of reuse issues. Booch (1987) is an excellent reference on the use of Ada in creating reusable software components; he emphasizes object-oriented design (OOD). EVB Software Engineering, Inc., markets a set of Ada software modules based on Booch's work (including components for stacks, lists, strings, queues, deques, rings, maps, sets, bags, trees, graphs, filters, pipes, sorting, searching, and pattern matching).

A recent issue of the *Ada Information Clearinghouse Newsletter* (AdaIC 1990), announced that the STARS program is now providing 33 reusable Ada components at no charge. Although the cost for each product was previously $50, the only cost now to the requestor is to provide either a 1/4-inch data cartridge or 9-track magnetic tape with each product request. Four tapes would be required for all the software. All media is copied using UNIX TAR format with a 6250 BPI magnetic tape, or a 1/4- inch data cartridge. The products include source code, test software, and documentation. They were produced by the Naval Research Laboratory (NRL) in cooperation with the

STARS program, as a base for further development. They are in the following STARS foundations technology areas: operating systems; database management systems; user interfaces; command language; graphics; text processing; network/communication; run-time support; planning and optimization; design, integration, and test; reusability assistance; and other areas. Included are such products as a prototype binding to the Structured Query Language (SQL), an interface to the X-Window system, and a symbolic debugger.

A STARS product listing may be requested, containing the name of each product, the company responsible for development, and a short abstract. For a copy of the product listing, contact:

> Naval Research Laboratory
> Attn: Code 5150
> Washington, DC 20375-5000

The products are also described in the *STARS Newsletter*, which also includes an order form. To receive a copy, contact:

> Managing Editor, STARS Newsletter
> Unisys Corporation
> Tactical Systems Division, Dept. 7670
> 12010 Sunrise Valley Drive
> Reston, VA 22091
> e-mail: newsletter@stars.reston.unisys.com

Vogelsong (1989) describes the status of the RAPID project. The goal of RAPID is to promote the reuse of Ada software and to reduce the cost of system development and maintenance. Developed for an 18-month pilot operational period (at the U.S. Army Information Systems Software Development Center in Falls Church, Virginia) by SofTech, under contract to ISEC, RAPID became operational May 1, 1989. During the first 9 months a single development effort was supported to prove reusability concepts, refine library software, and resolve contractual and management issues. During the remaining 9 months, the feasibility of servicing five Software Development Centers is to be assessed. The long-range plan is to include all of ISEC, Department of the Army, etc., as need and funding allow.

The initial RAPID domain analysis covered information management systems (financial, logistical, tactical management information, communication, personnel/force accounting, etc.), but the analysis is expected to expand to additional domains and to accommodate multiple projects. The RAPID Center Library (RCL) operates on a MicroVAX II and consists of 30,000 lines of Ada code. RAPID has a support staff to provide consultation on reuse throughout a project's life cycle. ISEC's experience with RAPID should be very valuable to other DOD segments as well as to other government and commercial organizations and universities.

A reuse project at Magnavox is described by Carstensen (1987). The U.S. Army Advanced Field Artillery Tactical Data System (AFATDS) project consisted of approximately 770,000 lines of Ada code, of which about 100,000 lines were reused code. Of the 100,000 lines, about 30,000 were reused unchanged and about 70,000 resulted from tailoring existing modules. Magnavox used OOD, which facilitated reuse. By way of incentive for reuse, at project initiation they determined and costed a specific software reuse factor that had to be met to stay on schedule and within budget. As Carstensen notes, this required acceptance of some risk by project-level management, and he emphasizes that whatever incentives are used, the single most important incentive (factor) is the acceptance by project management of any real or perceived risks associated with the reuse of previously developed software.

Selby (1989) studied software reuse activities at NASA Goddard Space Flight Center (GSFC). GSFC has active research projects in reuse and practices reuse. Selby considered 25 moderate and large-size software systems (from 3,000 to 112,000 lines of Fortran source code) that are support software for unmanned spacecraft control. The amount of software either reused or modified from previous systems averaged 32 percent per project. (Further details of Selby's study are given in section 3.3.6.) Subsequent efforts at GSFC with Ada code indicate reuse averages even higher than the 32 percent level experienced with Fortran code.

Lanergan and Grasso (1984) also emphasize the importance of management commitment in Raytheon's successful reuse project. The Information Processing Systems Organization of Raytheon's Missile Systems Division concluded that about 60 percent of their business application designs and code were redundant. By standardizing those functions in the form of reusable functional modules and logic structures, they are experiencing about a 50 percent gain in productivity. Also, they report marked improvement in the maintenance process due to a consistent style for all software, which permits the reassignment of personnel from maintenance to development of new systems.

Biggerstaff and Perlis (1989b) reprint the Lanergan and Grasso (1984) paper as well as papers by Prywes and Lock (1989) and Cavaliere (1989) on reuse in business applications. Prywes and Lock used a program generator approach, with results of a threefold gain in programmer productivity. Biggerstaff and Perlis observe that, while Cavaliere reports on an ad hoc approach at ITT Hartford Insurance, good results were obtained, largely because "the Hartford management supported, capitalized, and actively moved to assure the success of the project." Biggerstaff and Perlis also reprint and comment on papers by Oskarsson (1989) and Matsumoto (1989), who report reuse successes in telephony software and process control software, respectively. They note that reuse skeptics doubted the possibilities of reuse in these domains, since these domains impose unusually strict memory requirements and performance constraints. Matsumoto, of Toshiba, states that on average about one-half of the lines of code of their generated software products are reused code. With reuse at this level, their productivity (measured in lines of code per month) has increased more than 20 percent per year. Biggerstaff and Perlis note that these experiences reflect "what can be accomplished with enlightened and committed management coupled with existing technology." They suggest that a manager who is considering undertaking reuse should read about the experiences of these organizations (Biggerstaff and Perlis 1989b). Further details of the paper by Oskarsson is provided in section 3.2.6, and the paper by Cavaliere is further discussed in section 2.1.5.

Tracz (1987b) believes that the greatest payoff from reuse is realized in decreased maintenance costs. He reports maintenance cost reductions of up to 90 percent when reusable code, code templates, and application generators have been used to develop new systems.

While numerous organizations are achieving success in software reuse, not all organizations would be justified in making large investments in reuse because, for example, of the lack of commonality within their software projects (present and anticipated). We will consider this point further in later chapters.

1.5 Scope and Organization of this Book

The following chapters provide discussions of many management and technical issues pertaining to software reuse, including various approaches that have been used or suggested for dealing with the issues. We distill the suggestions into guidelines for use. While some of the guidelines are quite specific (e.g., those for programming in Ada), most are not. Recognizing that reuse is still a very new, evolving field, we offer the guidelines as suggestions only. We hope that the discussions and guidelines will be helpful in understanding the issues involved and will serve as a starting point for undertaking software reuse. Each organization involved should eventually establish its own set of guidelines.

In the next two chapters we consider reuse within the broad categories of managerial and technical approaches. Chapter 2 focuses on managerial aspects of reuse, giving consideration to some existing impediments to reuse and approaches to their resolution, to the creation of positive incentives for beginning and maintaining a reuse program, and to the important issue of instituting a software development and maintenance process incorporating reuse.

Chapter 3 focuses on technical aspects of reuse and provides approaches and guidelines covering the activities of domain analysis, preparing reusable components (spanning the entire software life cycle), ensuring component quality, and classifying and storing components. Specific guidelines are provided for developing Ada code modules for reuse. Approaches and guidelines for the reuse of software components are given, including searching, retrieving, understanding, assessing, adapting, and assembling components. Tools and environments for software reuse are also discussed.

Chapter 4, "Getting Started," contains some suggestions for a sequence of activities to implement reuse within an organization—from a modest beginning to a mature software reuse program. Carrying out the suggested activities of chapter 4 requires dealing with the issues to which the guidelines of chapters 2 and 3 apply.

Appendix A provides a complete list of the managerial and technical guidelines provided throughout this book. The technical guidelines are presented in Appendix A relative to the software life cycle. Appendix B provides guidelines for the reuse of Ada code. The book also includes an extensive bibliography as well as an index.

1.6 References

AdaIC June 1990. *Ada Information Clearinghouse Newsletter.* 8(2).

Anderson, C. M., and D. G. McNicholl. 1985. "Reusable Software—A Mission Critical Case Study." In *Proceedings of Compsac 85*, 205.

Barnes, B., T. Durek, J. Gaffney, and A. Pyster. July 1987a. "Cost Models for Software Reuse." In *Proceedings of the Tenth Minnowbrook Workshop (1987, Software Reuse)*. Blue Mountain Lake, N.Y.

Barnes, B., T. Durek, J. Gaffney, and A. Pyster. October 1987b. "A Framework and Economic Foundation for Software Reuse." In *Proceedings of the Workshop on Software Reuse*, ed. G. Booch and L. Williams. Rocky Mountain Inst. of Software Engineering, SEI, MCC, Software Productivity Consortium, Boulder, Colo.

Basili, V. R., H. D. Rombach, J. Bailey, and B. G. Joo. July 1987. "Software Reuse: A Framework." In *Proceedings of the Tenth Minnowbrook Workshop (1987, Software Reuse)*. Blue Mountain Lake, N.Y.

Biggerstaff, T. J. July 1989. "Design Recovery for Maintenance and Reuse." *Computer* **22**(7), 36–49.

Biggerstaff, T. J., and A. J. Perlis, ed. September 1984. "Special Issue on Software Reusability." *IEEE Trans. on Software Engr* **SE10**(5).

Biggerstaff, T. J., and A. J. Perlis, ed. 1989a. *Software Reusability. Concepts and Models*, vol. I, ACM Press, Addison-Wesley, Reading, Mass.

Biggerstaff, T. J., and A. J. Perlis, ed. 1989b. *Software Reusability. Applications and Experience*, vol. II, ACM Press, Addison-Wesley, Reading, Mass.

Biggerstaff, T. J., and C. Richter. March 1987. "Reusability Framework, Assessment, and Directions." *IEEE Software* 4(2), 41–49.

Bollinger, T. B. and S. L. Pfleeger. March 1990. "The Economics of Reuse: Issues and Alternatives." In *Proceedings of the Eighth Annual National Conference on Ada Technology*, 436–47. Atlanta, GA.

Booch, G. 1987. *Software Engineering With Ada*, 2nd ed. Benjamin/Cummings, Menlo Park, Calif.

Braun, C. L., J. B. Goodenough, and R. S. Eaves. April 1985. *Ada Reusability Guidelines*. U.S. Air Force ESD 3285-2-208/2.1, SofTech.

Carstensen, H. B., Jr. March 1987. "A Real Example of Reusing Ada Software." In *Proceedings of the Conference on Software Reusability and Maintainability*. The National Institute for Software Quality and Productivity, Inc., Tysons Corner, Va.

Cavaliere, M. J. 1989. "Reusable Code at the Hartford Insurance Group" In *Software Reusability. Applications and Experience*, vol. II, ACM Press, Addison-Wesley, Reading, Mass.

Conn, R. February 1986. "Overview of the DoD Ada Software Repository." *Dr. Dobb's Journal*, 60–61, 86–93.

Frakes, W. B., and B. A. Nejmeh. January 1987. "Software Reuse through Information Retrieval." In *Proceedings of the Twentieth Hawaii International Conference on System Sciences*, ed. B. D. Shriver and R. H. Sprague, Jr., 530–35. Kailua-Kona, Hawaii.

Freeman, P. 1987. *Tutorial: Software Reusability.* IEEE Computer Society.

Fujino, K. October 1987. "Software Factory Engineering: Today and Future." In *Proceedings of The 1987 Fall Joint Computer Conference,* 262–70. Dallas.

Guerrieri, E. March 1988. "Searching for Reusable Software Components with the Rapid Center Library System." In *Proceedings of the Sixth National Conference on Ada Technology,* 395–406. Arlington, Va.

Hall, P. A. V. 1988. "Software Components and Reuse." a special section in *Software Engineering Journal* **3**(5), 171.

Holibaugh, R. July 1989. "Reuse: Where to Begin and Why?" In *Proceedings of the Reuse in Practice Workshop,* ed. J. Baldo and C. Braun. Software Engineering Institute, Pittsburgh, Penn.

Hooper, J.W. and R.O. Chester. April 1990. *Software Reuse Guidelines.* U.S. Army AIRMICS ASQB-GI-90-015.

ISEC (U.S. Army Information Systems Engineering Command). December 1985. *ISEC Reusability Guidelines.* U.S. Army Information Systems Engineering Command 3285-4-247/2, Softech Inc., Waltham, Mass.

Jones, T. C. September 1984. "Reusability in Programming: A Survey of the State of the Art." *IEEE Trans. on Software Engr* **SE10**(5), 488–94.

Kang, K. C. October 1987. "A Reuse-Based Software Development Methodology." In *Proceedings of the Workshop on Software Reuse,* ed. G. Booch and L. Williams. Rocky Mountain Inst. of Software Engineering, SEI, MCC, Software Productivity Consortium, Boulder, Colo.

Lanergan, R. G., and C. A. Grasso. September 1984. "Software Engineering with Reusable Design and Code." *IEEE Trans. on Software Engr* **SE10**(5), 498–501.

Lubars, M. D. October 1987. "Wide-Spectrum Support for Software Reusability." In *Proceedings of the Workshop on Software Reuse,* ed. G. Booch and L. Williams. Rocky Mountain Inst. of Software Engineering, SEI, MCC, Software Productivity Consortium, Boulder, Colo.

Matsumoto, Y. 1989. "Some Experiences in Promoting Reusable Software: Presentation in Higher Abstract Levels." In *Software Reusability. Applications and Experience*, vol. II. ACM Press, Addison-Wesley, Reading, Mass.

McNicholl, D. G., et al. 1986. *Common Ada Missile Packages (CAMP), Vol I: Overview and Commonality Study Results.* AFATL-TR-85-93, McDonnell Douglas, St. Louis.

Oskarsson, O. 1989. "Reusability of Modules with Strictly Local Data and Devices–A Case Study" In *Software Reusability. Applications and Experience*, vol. II, ACM Press, Addison-Wesley, Reading, Mass.

Presson, P. E., J. Tsai, T. P. Bowen, J. V. Post, and R. Schmidt. July 1983. *Software Interoperability and Reusability Guidebook for Software Quality Measurement, vols. I and II.* Boeing Aerospace Co.

Prywes, N. S., and E. D. Lock. 1989. "Use of the Model Equational Language and Program Generator by Management Professionals" In *Software Reusability. Applications and Experience*, vol. II, ACM Press, Addison-Wesley, Reading, Mass.

Pyster, A., and B. Barnes. December 1987. *The Software Productivity Consortium Reuse Program.* SPC-TN-87-016, Software Productivity Consortium, Reston, Va.

St. Dennis, R. J. May 1986. *A Guidebook for Writing Reusable Source Code in Ada (R), Version 1.1.* CSC-86-3:8213, Honeywell, Golden Valley, Minn.

Selby, R. W. 1989. "Quantitative Studies of Software Reuse," In *Software Reusability: Vol. II Applications and Experience*, ed. T. J. Biggerstaff and A. J. Perlis, 213-33.

Tracz, W. July 1987a. "Making Reuse a Reality." *IEEE Software* 4(4).

Tracz, W. October 1987b. "Software Reuse Myths." In *Proceedings of the Workshop on Software Reuse*, ed. G. Booch and L. Williams. Rocky Mountain Inst. of Software Engineering, SEI, MCC, Software Productivity Consortium, Boulder, Colo.

Tracz, W. 1988a. "Ada Reusability Efforts: A Survey of the State of the Practice." In *Tutorial: Software Reuse: Emerging Technology*, 23–32. IEEE Computer Society.

Tracz, W. 1988b. *Tutorial. Software Reuse: Emerging Technology.* IEEE Computer Society.

Tracz, W. April 1990. "Where Does Reuse Start?" *ACM Software Eng. Notes* **15**(2), 42-46.

Vogelsong, T. July 1989. "Reusable Ada Packages for Information System Development (RAPID) – An operational Center of Excellence for Software Reuse." In *Proceedings of the Reuse in Practice Workshop*, ed. J. Baldo and C. Braun. Software Engineering Institute, Pittsburgh, Penn.

Wald, E. 1986. *STARS Reusability Guidebook, V4.0* (Draft). U.S. Department of Defense, STARS.

Wegner, P. July 1984. "Capital-Intensive Software Technology." *IEEE Software* **1**(3).

Managerial Guidelines

There are those who argue that the only significant impediments to successful software reuse are technical in nature; and, some argue that if only we can solve the management problems, we can achieve success in reuse. We are of the opinion that serious consideration must be given to both technical and managerial issues in order to achieve success—much as is true for software engineering in general. Lack of attention to either management or technical issues would almost certainly result in failure. We thus focus on the managerial issues in this chapter, and deal with technical issues in chapter 3.

In this chapter we consider some of the issues an organization's management must face to be successful in software reuse. Section 2.1 considers such issues as management approaches and organization; behavioral issues; and contractual, legal, and financial considerations. An overview of the software reuse program at Hartford Insurance, including the management approaches tasken, is presented. Section 2.2 discusses integrating reuse into the software development and maintenance process. An overview of the reuse-based process plan of the DOD Joint Integrated Avionics Working Group (JIAWG) is presented.

2.1 Managerial Issues and Approaches

Many issues must be resolved to achieve a successful software reuse program. There are organizational, economic, legal, and sociological issues (Fairley et al. 1989) as well as issues of technology transfer, politics, tradition, and the continual advancement of technology (Aharonian 1989). Some technical reuse issues need to be resolved as well. The exact nature of issues will vary from one organization to another. Thus solutions to issues must be tailored to each organization. For example, DOD agencies have different legal issues to face than do their contractors. Thus we consider a broad spectrum of issues, with suggestions for eliminating (or alleviating) disincentives and for introducing incentives.

17

2.1.1 Organizational Management and Structure

Top-level management must take positive action to make software reuse a reality. This means much more than just issuing an edict that software reuse will occur. It means committing the resources necessary to bring about a different way of approaching software development and maintenance—including a different process, tools, a well-trained staff, and an adequate initial library of reusable components. It means spending seed money for later gains. Management must be prepared to wait for the investment to begin earning returns. Realistic goals must be set, and risks must be accepted.

Biggerstaff and Perlis (1989b) observe that the introduction of a new technology is costly, is perceived as disruptive, and is often difficult to retrofit to existing systems. Rather than face such difficulties, organizations may look elsewhere for "magic solutions," including emphasizing better management. While such an emphasis is important, it should not be done to the exclusion of technical improvements. Biggerstaff and Perlis note that some very simple technical improvements could help a great deal in most organizations—improving the reusability of software and vastly improving the productivity and quality of software development in general. They bemoan the poor environments often available to programmers and designers and say that "if our agricultural system were capitalized at an analogous level, we would still be an agrarian society struggling to feed our population." They continue as follows:

> Recent studies have shown that the two easiest ways to improve software development productivity and quality (in general) are to (1) capitalize the programmers/designers with fully loaded workstations and environments (one per programmer/designer) and (2) put programmer/designers in soundproof offices so that they can close out the interference and concentrate on the work at hand. In other words, capitalize them to do their job. The steps that enhance the productivity and quality of programming in general also enhance the reusability of the resulting software.

Biggerstaff and Perlis (1989b) observe that the successful reuse projects summarized in the book all had in common the commitment of management—including capitalization and active guidance and involvement to ensure success. They provide the following recommendations based on the various experiments in reuse reported in their book:

1. Capitalize your developmental programmers with the fullest and best resources (workstations, tools, environments, and offices).
2. Establish organizational standards for design, reuse, and programming. Once those standards are validated on a reasonably large scale,
3. Enforce them over the whole development organization.
4. Get management's commitment to make the whole thing work by fostering a climate where good practices and reuse are rewarded, and the alternatives are not.
5. Concurrently, establish research and development organizations whose missions are to explore new technologies that extend your existing development standards, tools, environments, and technologies to improve the payoff and answer similar moves by the competition.

Fairley et al. (1989) examined six successful software reuse projects and observed that in all of the projects support was provided by upper management.

Technical personnel must know that management is firmly committed to reuse, that perfunctory efforts are not acceptable, and that success in reuse will bring positive career rewards. Too many good new ideas die within organizations because management expects technical personnel to carry all the burden, including work over and above usual duties, with little or no support from management and sometimes with only negative incentives. One can guarantee that software reuse will never really flourish if the burden is on technical personnel alone. They simply cannot accommodate the necessary efforts to achieve success in reuse unless management provides resources and realistic assignments that take into account the expectation of reuse activities.

Top-level management must initiate planning and decision making for reuse, including decisions on scope for reuse (what organizational components will be involved, what life-cycle phases will be supported, and what application areas will be addressed). Organizational structure and behavior must be addressed. Contractual and financial approaches likely will be necessary. A decision with major implications is which process the organization will use for software development and maintenance (see section 2.2). Training in software reuse must be provided to managers as well as to technical personnel, and recruitment of a few strategic professionals may be advisable. Technical and managerial personnel should be rewarded for achievements in reuse.

Managers in government organizations are in an especially strong position to bring about reuse—not only in-house but on the part of their contractors. There are currently substantial difficulties to overcome, as we will discuss in the following subsections, but markedly improved software productivity and quality are the prospective results of the undertaking. The best motivator for both management and technical personnel will be witnessing success. To that end it is very important that management carefully plan a reuse program before initiating it, including choice of early projects that seem likely to have a good payoff from reuse.

Tracz (1990) discusses the reuse roles of different kinds of personnel, noting that software reuse is a people issue as well as a technology issue and that a number of the important participants have non-technical roles. He stresses the importance of top management requiring that reuse be carried out and overcoming the reluctance of an individual project manager to invest effort and money for the benefit of a later project. He mentions several companies that set goals for reuse on new projects and for contributions of products to the reuse library. For example, one company's top management has set a reuse ratio goal of 20 percent on all new projects and a contribution ratio of 5 percent (subject to approval of the Reuse Committee). In this way, mid-level managers are motivated to achieve reuse, as are programmers. Tracz suggests that systems analysts should be used in conducting domain analyses.

Tracz emphasizes the importance of educators teaching students how to achieve reuse, including such topics as domain analysis, application generator construction, and parameterized programming. He mentions that tool developers may be able to play a role, but he does not see the need for "exotic and elaborate" tools to support reuse. He notes that a customer can insist on reuse and, especially in the case of DOD, can be effective in doing so. He also observes that a salesperson who knows the marketplace and recognizes the potential for reusable software could help build the business case to justify the capitalization of reusable software.

Myers (1990) summarized a case study (given by John Favaro of the European Consultants Network) regarding reuse conducted at Intecs Sistemi in Pisa, Italy. Favaro was surprised to find that engineers were very willing to attempt to use components from a repository that they had not designed or implemented. He was more surprised to learn the reason for their cooperativeness: "They thought it would be easy." Favaro concluded that a contributing factor was the low level of training in modern software engineering concepts among the engineers; they had little if any prior knowledge about abstract data types, genericity, and OOD. He believes there is far too little appreciation within the software engineering community of the intrinsic technical difficulty of reuse.

Curtis (1989) concludes that the need for programmers and analysts with specialized skills will not be reduced by the availability of reusable artifacts. Reusable artifacts will be helpful primarily to experienced programmers who can distinguish among several components with similar functionality. Also software reuse will increase emphasis on design, interface control, and system testing, which require skilled programmers. Further, reuse will decrease emphasis on coding and module testing, thus decreasing the need for less experienced programmers. Belady (1989) has stated that "reusability is the best manifestation of software engineering industrialized, and ... the software engineer is becoming less the programmer and more the system designer."

Fairley et al. (1989) have researched how to organize software reuse. They discuss functional, matrix, and project approaches, and conclude that the best approach is a "reuse matrix" structure with domain-specific reuse groups. One or more individuals from domain reuse groups would be assigned to each project as a reuse "facilitator" for software relating to his/her domain of expertise. Each domain reuse group would be responsible for maintaining a library of reusable components, for educating and assisting other programmers in the use of components available from the domain, and for encouraging the creation of additional reusable software.

Section 2.1.5 discusses the management approaches taken in the successful software reuse efforts at the Hartford Insurance Group, including formation of a project team and a review board. In section 2.2.5 we summarize the management approach taken in the DOD JI-AWG reuse program and also describe their overall software process based on reuse.

The following guidelines summarize some recommendations; some are from Fairley et al.

MS1: *Upper-level management must set reuse goals, create an organizational infrastructure to support software reuse, establish policies, and provide necessary resources.*

MS2: *Mid-level management must develop procedures, populate the organizational structure, allocate resources, and establish controls and metrics to achieve goals.*

MS3: *Project-level management and technical personnel must carry out the reuse/reusability activities in individual projects.*

MS4: *Establish an organizational entity whose charter is to promote reuse considerations at the corporate level.*

MS5: *Evaluate the suitability of establishing the reuse matrix structure and domain reuse groups.*

MS6: *Structure software development by domains amenable to reuse considerations.*

MS7: *Establish strong connections between reuse and maintenance activities.*

MS8: *Provide different types of training for managers, developers, and domain reuse specialists.*

MS9: *Make personnel assignments that take reuse and reusability into account.*

MS10: *Assign reuse facilitators to development groups.*

MS11: *Allow two to three years after initiating software reuse before expecting economic advantages from the program.*

MS12: *Provide a corporate financial "safety net" for projects practicing reuse; provide funding for generation of reusable components.*

MS13: *Managers in federal organizations must take the initiative to influence the adoption of reuse within their own organizations and within contracts they direct.*

MS14: *Be realistic. Do not promise too much, too soon.*

2.1.2 Organizational Behavior

A number of disincentives discourage personnel from cooperating in using available existing software and in preparing and supplying their own products for use by others. Fairley et al. (1989) mention some disincentives to using reusable components: "not invented here" syndrome, more "fun" to build than adapt, differing styles and quality criteria, and technical constraints on the product. They mention the following as disincentives to contributing reusable components: schedule constraints, stylistic issues, reward structure, and peer pressure. They also strongly emphasize the importance of reuse being a corporate concern, with impetus for reuse coming from top-level management; i.e., a corporate culture must be established that emphasizes reuse. Fairley et al. examined six successful reuse projects, and observed that in all of them, practicing reuse had become almost a "way of life".

To encourage individuals to participate effectively in reuse activities, one approach is to provide behavioral incentives, such as sharing cost savings, time off, bonuses, free dinners, reserved parking, public awards, and reuse bonus points. More effective, according to Fairley et al. (1989), is to seek to enhance psychological job satisfaction to motivate willing participation in reuse. Examples they suggest are: to provide corporate-level support for reuse as a meaningful endeavor; to reuse work products at higher levels of abstraction than code; to define carefully reuse roles for all involved personnel; to determine job performance through a metrics program; to provide for professional growth through job rotation and skills acquisition; to practice information hiding and object-oriented development to provide some autonomy; and to emphasize/train to give and accept constructive criticism. Fairley et al. make the important point that many of these approaches to enhance participation in reuse also promote good software engineering practices. In the successful reuse projects examined by Fairley et al., reuse was such a "way of life" that little emphasis or direct management incentives were needed to encourage developers.

The above suggestions are briefly summarized in the following guidelines.

OB1: *Provide incentive rewards to participate in reuse.*

OB2: *Seek to enhance psychological job satisfaction to motivate willing participation in reuse.*

2.1.3 Contractual and Legal Considerations

Substantial disincentives regarding software reuse exist relative to contracting arrangements and ownership rights. Cost-Plus contracts currently provide disincentives to contractors to make use of reusable products. In fact, they provide incentives to redevelop rather than to reuse. Firm Fixed Price (FFP) contracts are worse regarding creation of reusable products—at least for delivery to the customer— since preparing products for reuse costs extra money. There might be motivation to reuse available products (if such existed) in an FFP contract, as this could lead to greater profit. It could also be, of course, that effort could be expended under internal company funds to generalize some software developed under the contract for the company's later advantage.

The government must make it attractive to companies to create reusable software and to reuse software by providing incentives. A suggestion is to provide incentives through extra awards for contributions to, or applications of, reuse as value engineering similar to the hardware program (Joiner 1989). Companies could be required (or encouraged) to address applicable reusable software in submitted proposals. Contract reviews should include the status of reuse efforts. If such changes in government procurement policy are to be made, then accompanying changes must occur in how government projects are funded. At present no funds are allocated to a project to prepare software components for future use.

It appears that a company must always retain some proprietary software for competitive advantage. To the extent software is placed in a repository for general use, a company must be duly compensated for the expected loss of revenue that retention of the software would have provided; i.e., royalties must be paid. Hall (1987) mentions the idea of a "meter" within a software component, that counts uses, and charges accordingly. Clearly DOD and other agencies must resolve the legal and contracting issues involved for the national benefit.

Baker and Deeds (1989) argue that the government should not attempt to establish libraries of reusable software except in the cases in which a government organization does its own software development. They also raise the issue of the government's liability in the case of government-furnished software. They believe that government libraries will tend toward obsolescence because the government has less incentive than industry to maintain state-of-the-art libraries. They further state:

> Government should not tell corporations how to reuse software or make them use governmental libraries. If reuse makes sense, they will do it. They do not need us to make them do this. Double-billing for reused software should be ameliorated by increased competition and increased emphasis on establishing productivity baselines and measures.

There do seem to be situations, however, in which the government should build up libraries of contractor-developed software. One situation is a large project in which a number of contractors are involved and in which each contractor depends on a common subset of software. An example is strategic defense, in which many contractors are developing software, and without a government-held library, much duplication will likely occur.

There are several levels at which the government can promote reuse and reusability:

1. Encourage reuse internally in a government organization, where its library is integrated with its software process (section 2.2).
2. In a contract with a single company, encourage reuse and reusability by procurement policy, but let the company decide how technically to handle library and process.
3. In a contract (or related contracts) spanning multiple companies, encourage sharing by procurement policy, as well as company-internal reuse; in this case it may be necessary for the government to establish a government-managed reuse library to serve the group of companies.

One issue relating to libraries serving multiple companies is that if software components other than code are reused, they may be tied to a specific software process of the company that created the components, and thus might be unwieldy for use by other companies. For example, designs based on functional decomposition and designs based on the object-oriented approach could be awkward to integrate. Here again the government may influence the process to some extent by procurement policy.

The DOD JIAWG reuse initiative is addressing both contractual and legal issues within a federal government context. A brief summary is given in Reifer (1990), along with references to related documents. This program is in the planning stage at present. Section 2.2.5 discusses the DOD JIAWG modifications of DOD-STD-2167A to incorporate reuse activities.

It is clear that some changes are necessary to the government procurement process to encourage reuse and reusability. The *STARS Reusability Guidebook* (Wald 1986) appears to be the most complete coverage of the government procurement process relative to reuse prepared to date. Many legal issues are as yet unresolved pertaining to software reuse, particularly those concerning ownership rights to software (for example, when developed under contract to the government) and liabilities for errors when software is reused by other organizations. These issues may be resolved by legislation, by stipulations of individual contracts, or by the results of litigation over time. More research is needed to formulate specific recommendations for resolving this important issue.

The above observations lead us to the following guidelines.

CL1: *Seek contractual means to require or to encourage contractors to create reusable software (from which the government gains future benefits) and to reuse existing software (which gives the government immediate benefits).*

CL2: *Establish and enforce reuse practices within government development groups.*

CL3: *Require reuse within a group of related contracts (e.g., by a prime contractor and subcontractors).*

CL4: *Seek means to alter project funding approaches to encourage creation of reusable software.*

CL5: *Seek resolution to the legal issues of potential liability and partial ownership.*

2.1.4 Financial Considerations

It costs more to prepare software for reuse than for a single use because of the extra effort required to generalize and to test the components, to document them well, and to classify and retain them for reuse. If reuse is to be successful, an organization must be willing to "capitalize" or fund library mechanisms and an initial library of reusable components.

Biggerstaff and Perlis (1989a) note similarities between capitalization in the industrial revolution and the role of capitalization in software technology. They indicate that the lack of capitalization in the software industry may result from three factors: (a) financial approaches of companies have not adapted to the necessity for high capitalization of software development, (b) many companies do not yet realize the importance of software to their future products and profits, and (c) it takes a long time for companies to make use of existing technology successes (such as workstations and development environments), and even longer for such advanced technologies as reuse. They draw a parallel with the steel industry, suggesting that those companies that recognize the growing importance of software in their competitive position and capitalize it aggressively are more likely to survive than those that do not. They cite the aggressive capitalization of software development by the Japanese, emphasizing reuse, as enhancing their competitive position. Biggerstaff and Perlis make the observation that time will not be kind to nonaggressive companies and industries. Clearly, capitalization is necessary for reuse to succeed—and there are already examples of reuse leading to significant improvements in productivity and quality of software where management commitment and capitalization are present. Burton et al. (1987) state that a significant outcome of their reuse project was a change in management's view of software productivity. Software development is now viewed as the production of a long-lived corporate asset rather than as an isolated effort to meet a single deliverable.

Wegner (1984) urges the capitalization of software technology. He states:

> Many of us who work in the field of software technology feel that the 1980s are more exciting then the 1970s and that the 1990s may prove to be even more so. Living in a period of rapid technological change provides both an opportunity and a responsibility for shaping the future. It requires us to be more innovative and to take greater risks than in a period of greater stability. But worthwhile progress can be achieved only by taking some risks, making some hard decisions, and investing in the future.

In order to assess opportunities for reuse and reusability, cost predictions must be made. Barnes et al. (1987) present a framework for analyzing reuse cost. Underlying the costing must be a database of financial data on previous projects. Unfortunately most organizations have no such record of project performance data, but one can be built over time.

While there are several cost models in use for the general software process, only recently has work been done in cost modeling for reuse/reusability assessment. As part of the AIRMICS Ada Reuse and Metrics project, George Mason University and CONTEL Technology Center surveyed available software cost models relative to reuse, and prepared an extensive bibliography (see Fairley et al. 1989). They concluded that Ada-COCOMO is the best available cost model for modeling Ada development. The model incorporates costs for developing reusable components and savings from reusing components. The model also incorporates incremental development as an option. A major shortcoming of Ada-COCOMO is that it models reuse on a project-by-project basis. In fact, the researchers could find no existing cost model that treats reuse as an organizational issue rather than a project-level issue. Fairley et al. (1989) recommend the use of Ada-COCOMO in the short term, with development of economic models/cost models at the corporate level, in the longer term.

Bollinger and Pfleeger (1990) discuss various aspects of a software cost estimation model developed specifically to deal with decisions about software reuse. Their expectation is that, if developers are able to assess the impact of creating reusable parts on a current project and then predict the value of the reuse of those components on future projects, the production of reusable components can become a standard activity during software development. In their opinion, any cost estimation methodology that acknowledges software reuse must address the following set of foundation concepts:

- Baseline Projects
- Producer/Consumer View of Reuse
- Broad Spectrum Reuse
- Cost Factors

We summarize some of their comments on these concepts.

A set of projects within a particular application area often will involve the same or similar development activities, use similar development environments, and involve development teams with similar performance and experience histories. Thus the resulting productivity and costs tend to be similar also. Managers who are experienced in a given application area often use intuition to make cost estimates for a new project in the application area simply by noting how the project is likely to differ from past projects. This idea of estimation based on changes to a known development effort is central to evaluation of reuse, since reuse benefits must be measured in terms of an equivalent project without reuse. The known development effort is termed a "baseline project", and is used as a reference point for the estimation. Bollinger and Pfleeger assume that the baseline project explicitly represents cost in a form amenable to automated support and analysis.

A baseline project cost framework contains two types of cost components: (a) stable development components, which may be represented by fixed costs, such as procurements or developments where the costs are accurately predictable; and (b) variable development components in which something new is being developed and whose costs must be based on labor rates and production rates. The authors suggest representing costs of development by diagrams in which stable development components are represented by blocks and variable development components are represented by drawings of clouds. They decompose the diagrams to lower levels until the granularity is adequate from a risk standpoint. For example, a cloud could be decomposed into some blocks and clouds, where the blocks are stable; then the remaining clouds can be further decomposed, etc. Any components whose cost behaviors are very well understood could perhaps be represented by a single-level diagram.

Bollinger and Pfleeger provide an economic framework for assessing reuse cost impacts. They characterize reusable component developers as "producers," and the users of such components are called "consumers." Producers incur the initial cost and receive little or no benefit from their reuse efforts, and consumers take advantage of the work products—although they must understand, retrieve, and adapt the components. Of course, consumers and producers could be the same individuals, but the distinction is important for understanding and modeling the costs involved.

A significant inhibitor of reuse no doubt is the lack of incentive strategies for encouraging reuse investments. As these authors point out, without such incentives the best we can hope for is "scavenging" existing products, in which case each consumer bears the full cost of finding, understanding and modifying the work products to meet a project's needs. Especially with code scavenging, this is a very expensive way to operate, and even more so if the personnel involved are unfamiliar with the original design or use of the products. This stands in sharp contrast to well planned up-front investment in reusable components that are easier to find and use; such planning should result in subsequent projects requiring much less effort and involving much less risk than development from scratch.

It is clear that management must play an active role in encouraging and investing in reuse to bring about effective producing and consuming relationships. Bollinger and Pfleeger refer to reuse investments (the cost to make work products reusable) and reuse benefits (the difference between the cost to develop without reuse and the cost to reuse). For any given reusable component, the total reuse benefit is the sum of the cost benefits of all instances of reuse, less the reuse investment for the component.

Bollinger and Pfleeger discuss the paradox that faces management in considering reuse: for any given project, reuse investments are excess costs to that project, and are optional costs as well—they are not necessary to successful completion of the project and may, in fact, delay project completion. Realistically, then, it is necessary for a manager to justify a reuse investment by accurately predicting the expected reuse benefit. That is, in order to realize a benefit, the investment in a component, plus the adaptation costs for all instances of reuse for the component, must be less than the cost of developing the software for all the instances without reusing the component. Effective cost modeling tools are necessary for such estimates.

Bollinger and Pfleeger discuss the importance of reusing work products and knowledge from all life-cycle phases (broad-spectrum reuse), noting that reuse of products from the earlier activities of the software development process can provide benefits far greater than the development cost of the items. This additional benefit is due to the "inclusion effect"—the use of such a work product explicitly mandates or implicitly includes the use of subsequent work products. For example, the reuse of a design module may allow the reuse of the corresponding code. The authors point out that development of tools to facilitate reuse of early phase products holds great promise for increasing levels of reuse. Also they mention the need for cost models to assess the "ripple effects" resulting from reuse at various stages in the software development process.

The authors refer to a "cost factor," which means any identifiable feature of a new project that is likely to change significantly one or more of the nominal costs of the baseline project. The scope of a cost factor is the full set of development components affected by the ripple effect of the cost factor on subsequent development components. They note that the scope of a cost factor will encompass any inclusion effects of reuse, thus making cost estimation of such effects explicit.

A customer for whom software is developed has no economic interest, in general, for making any components of the software reusable. The reason is, of course, that the customer would not expect to receive any benefit from the investment. An exception would be when the customer is also the developer. The general solution is to distribute costs over a collection of projects by means of an amortization schedule. The developer may invest some internal funds on making a component reusable, and be reimbursed later by other projects that reuse the component. These authors encourage research to identify candidate amortization schemes and the situations in which they would be most appropriate. They encourage modeling consumer reuse as a procurement activity that is similar to the purchase of commercial software packages, rather than as a productivity issue (i.e., rather than considering component functionality or size). Thus the cost to a reusing project would depend upon the pricing scheme determined earlier by the producer.

Bollinger and Pfleeger discuss the idea of making amortization and pricing decisions based on the concept of cost sharing domains (CSDs) in which present and future project costs can be added together and treated as a unit value. A CSD thus would be a set of development organizations likely to use a particular set of reusable components; but the organizations must be related in some manner that permits equitable distribution of cost. Examples of such CSD mechanisms given by the authors are (a) the commercial sale of software, with all purchasers being part of the CSD; (b) the use of a joint capital expense pool by several projects; and (c) consortia consisting of multiple companies that create a mechanism for sharing costs of developing tools or technologies for use by all the member companies.

The authors also present the idea of a CSD bank, an entity that provides initial capital for building reusable products—i.e., makes reuse investment loans. This could take many forms, including a commercial bank if a convincing case could be made for the viability of the investment. They view the CSD bank as being the owner of all reusable resources (forming the CSD resource pool) and expect the bank to charge customers for use of the products it has helped to fund.

The authors speak of the "reuse cost cycle" that results when the concepts of reuse investments, reuse producers, reuse consumers, CSDs, CSD banks, reuse investment loans, and CSD resource pools are combined. They say that the CSD bank should perhaps in some cases be an actual staffed function that requires applications for reuse investment loans be made and reviewed. Another approach is a "distributed barter economy" in which employees invest free time in hopes of later cash payment for each use of their components. The CSD boundaries could be within a single project, across several related projects within one company, across an entire company, over a number of companies via a consortium, or over a very large base of companies and personnel when costs are shared by offering a reusable product for sale on the commercial market.

These authors have developed the "delta cost estimation" method based on these concepts, and give a reference to another paper that describes that work.

Myers (1990) summarized comments by John Favaro of the European Consultants Network. Favaro applied an economic model of reuse developed by the Software Productivity Consortium (SPC), including such variables as the percentage of code contributed by reusable components, the cost of integrating the component rather than developing it from scratch, the charge to use a component from a repository, and the cost of making a component reusable. He classified components in terms of complexity. The relative cost of integrating components ranged from 1.10 for the simplest component to 1.63 for the most complex. The relative cost of reusable component production ranged from 1.20 to 4.80. The payoff threshold values (i.e., number of uses required to amortize development cost) varied from 1.33 to 12.97. His conclusion was that the least complex components would be amortized after approximately two uses, medium-complexity components would require three to four uses for amortization, while the most complex components would require from six to thirteen uses. While Favaro does not contend that these figures are precisely correct, he does believe they are sufficiently valid that expectations of early payoff from reusable component development may need to be revised upward.

We offer the following guidelines on reuse financial considerations.

F1: *Establish mechanisms to accumulate an organizational database of historical financial data relative to software production and maintenance, including reuse activities.*

F2: *Provide cost-modeling tools, to the extent feasible, in concert with organizational data for reuse/reusability decision assessments (including make versus reuse versus buy decisions).*

F3: *Consider/model costs over multiple projects.*

F4: *Establish mechanisms to share the cost of developing reusable components across multiple projects.*

2.1.5 Case Study: Reuse Program at Hartford Insurance Group

Cavaliere (1983) reports on the reuse efforts at the Hartford Insurance Group. Their approach to getting started in reuse was to form a project team (The Reusable Code Project) to address the issue of reusable code with the following main objectives:

- to develop and implement a procedure for collecting and communicating reusable code and techniques;
- to promote awareness and acceptance of reusable code as an effective productivity tool by the data processing staff;
- to assess and recommend long-term support requirements for reusable code, including training, tools, techniques, and management support.

They defined "reusable code" as any technique that increases productivity by eliminating redundant practices in program generation. Cavaliere cites reduced program creation time and a consequent reduction in resource consumption as the net advantages of reuse. Also testing is benefitted, since the code being reused has already been tested, thus the focus of testing can be on the newly coded areas of a program/system. Errors stemming from code interdependence are reduced because reusable program routines by their nature foster greater independence among logic functions. Cavaliere also observes that reusable code boosts program quality, thus less time and resources are required for maintenance. Also programmers who are new to the application benefit from reusable components that are similar in design and structure.

Hartford's efforts pertained primarily to COBOL programs. They implemented program skeletons for reuse (ensuring uniformity of baseline code relative to company standards); logic structures (i.e., code templates containing high-level code for application areas to which application-specific low-level code is added to develop a complete program); modules that cross application boundaries (e.g., date validation, numeric-to-text conversion); code generators (e.g., a working storage generator that reads in a formatted report and generates the COBOL working storage division entries needed in a program producing that report); and various operating system command sequences.

To promote the first project objective listed above (collecting and communicating reusable code and techniques), Hartford established a Reusable Code Review Board. This board consists of one member from each of the company's application programming divisions. Their responsibilities include

- encouraging members of their division to submit suggestions for reusable code that needs to be developed or for existing code that should be publicized,
- reviewing code suggestions for usefulness and quality,
- helping to refine code accepted from the divisions,
- assisting in the piloting of new software facilities,
- demonstrating reusable code facilities and answering questions on their use.

Cavaliere states that the board is of great value in transferring techniques and tools of code reuse to actual users and in ensuring that reusable code and tools are being made available that answer real needs in the application areas.

Also to promote the objective of collection and communication, Hartford established an on-line code catalog (which performs searches based on user-specified words or phrases); asked that reusability assessments be made during the software inspection process conducted for all programs that are released for production use (for follow-up by the appropriate review board member); and established a recognition program. Incentive to submit ideas/code to the review board is provided by mementos (that feature a reusable code logo), public recognition from upper management, and cash awards for reusable code suggestions.

The second objective of the program, promoting reuse awareness and acceptance, was promoted by

- publishing both general information and detailed articles about reusable code regularly in the Data Processing departmental newsletter,
- presenting concepts and options regarding reusable code to each basic programming training class,

- publicizing new releases of code via bulletin boards and the on-line index.

The third objective (establishing long-term support environments) was encouraged by making reusable code readily available on-line for incorporation into software being developed and by establishing a Data Processing Resource Center, staffed by professionals to solve problems, answer questions, provide support, and coordinate activities of the Reusable Code Review Board.

Cavaliere observes that there has been some difficulty in obtaining suitable modules for refinement and release as common modules, and that more time and resources than originally anticipated have been required to develop modules into clean, generic, supportable units for reuse. However, he says that the modules that have been implemented are proving valuable enough to warrant the necessary effort. He says there remains a tendency for programmers to copy known modules, modifying them to suit new specifications, rather than using program skeletons. However, providing appropriate logic structures has helped reduce the reliance on older, less-standard modules. He also notes that maximizing availability of a varied set of tools in an ever-changing operational environment requires significant ongoing time and effort.

Cavaliere indicates that research is underway at Hartford in the reuse of design and specification information (both textual and graphic) and component composition possibilities inherent in the OOD approach.

Based upon Hartford's experience in instituting reusable code methods and practices in their large data processing organization, Cavaliere offers the following recommendations:

- Utilize tendencies among staff members to develop code-generation tools oriented to the organization's needs. Not only do fourth-generation tools speed development of code, such tools help bring about a code inventory with standardized style and structure—resulting in improved maintainability.
- Develop and maintain an automated index of all programs released into production; include brief, precise, functional descriptions—which could be obtained automatically from comments supplied in the source code. This may be of value in identifying existing, potentially reusable code and in identifying redundant application functions that may imply a need for new reusable code.
- Be prepared to make full-time staff resources available for the start-up phase and for ongoing support of a reusability program.

- Provide resources to measure productivity effects of reuse compared against a baseline; this is important to assess the value of reuse and to justify the necessary resource commitment.
- Seek mechanisms for sharing reuse experiences and ideas (e.g., workshops, conferences, and working groups).

Biggerstaff and Perlis (1989b), commenting on the success of reuse at Hartford Insurance, say that the company's ad-hoc approach yielded good results. In their opinion the success of the project was largely a result of the Hartford management's support, capitalization, and actions to ensure the success of the project—an example of what can be accomplished with enlightened and committed management coupled with existing technology.

2.2 Software Development and Maintenance Incorporating Reuse

2.2.1 The Software Process

Humphrey (1989) suggests the following definitions:

- Software refers to a program and all of the associated information and materials needed to support its installation, operation, repair, and enhancement.
- Software engineering refers to the disciplined application of engineering, scientific, and mathematical principles and methods to the economical production of quality software.
- The software engineering process is the total set of software engineering activities needed to transform a user's requirements into software.

Humphrey comments that the software engineering process may include, as appropriate, requirements specification, design, implementation, verification, installation, operational support, and documentation as well as temporary or long-term repair and/or enhancement (i.e., maintenance) to meet continuing needs. There is a great deal of research relative to this process, as evidenced by the ongoing Software Process Workshops (e.g., Tully 1989). The issues we considered in section 2.1 (e.g., management approaches and cost modeling) all pertain to the software process incorporating reuse.

As Wegner (1984) and others have pointed out, uniformity of process is very important for success in software reuse; it supports the development of standard methodologies and tools. Wegner also notes the importance of standardizing major software subsystems such as communications, databases and workstations. He mentions some disadvantages of Ada as a basis for reusable components, but notes that one of the strongest arguments for Ada is that the mere existence of a standard is more important than the product on which to standardize—thus providing economic benefits from common subroutine libraries and a common environment. Clearly Ada alone cannot bring about reuse, however. Biggerstaff and Perlis (1989a) make the following observations:

> We have resisted the temptation to cast reuse into a strictly language paradigm. That is, we have not taken the position that some language, say Ada, is the answer to all or most reuse issues. Such a position implies that there are no further problems to be solved, or if there are, they are trivially simple. Some people do take a position that is almost as radical as this, but we believe that such an approach misses all of the deep issues and hard problems in reuse and in the end will exploit very little of the significant productivity and quality opportunities that reuse can provide.

A major impediment to reuse of software has been a mindset of always thinking in terms of new development. The software processes used in most organizations do not even take reuse into account. And organizations that emphasize reuse may not have reuse activities well integrated with the software development and maintenance process. It is becoming very clear that if reuse is to occur in an effective way, it must be integrated into the software process in such a way that we consider reusing software as the means to satisfy requirements before we consider developing new software.

An article entitled "Learning about Japan in Atlanta" (AdaIC 1990) discusses Dr. Sholom Cohen's tutorial "Designing for Reuse," which was presented at the Eighth Annual National Conference on Ada Technology in Atlanta in March 1990. Cohen (of SEI) defined reuse as "the process of implementing new software systems from pre-existing software." He discussed the "Japanese Software Factory" approach in which the factory tells clients what kinds of functions and programs are available. If a client wants to deviate from the off-the-shelf software, the estimate for the project usually goes up to two or three times the cost of using reusable modules. The result is that clients' programs are half built from existing code, on average.

The major difference between the Japanese and American methods of developing software, according to Cohen, is that most American software developers assume the role of a waiter equipped with no menu: they greet each customer with, "What would you like for dinner?" If the diner happens to ask for a dish that is already prepared, that is an unexpected bonus. Cohen observed that American software developers act just as pleased when their client's "order" happens to correspond to available reusable modules. We would agree with Cohen that currently software developers would be especially pleased, since the same price is likely to be charged to the customer regardless of whether available software is reused. Changes are certain to occur in pricing approaches as reuse becomes more common. In contrast to the American approach, the Japanese present a menu of the house specialties. The expectation is that the "order" (i.e., requirements) will be molded around what is available. While the exact reuse-based productivity gains of the Japanese "Software Factories" are somewhat difficult to validate, there is no doubt that the approach they use can improve productivity. Their approach consists of emphasizing rather narrow application domains, attempting first to reuse existing software, and finally developing new software as a last resort.

DOD-STD-2167A guides development of software for the government. Taylor (1989) has correctly observed, "Although the practices detailed in this standard do not preclude extensive use of software components, the life-cycle model and data requirements provide little support for or active encouragement of software component technology." The problem is no doubt more fundamental than the DOD standard, per se, in that if most government and industrial organizations practice reuse at all, it is in an ad hoc, nonsystematic way. Each organization needs a systematic approach to the development and maintenance of software that includes reuse and reusability as important, integral, natural, and inescapable elements.

2.2.2 Life-Cycle Models

The waterfall model, inherent in DOD-STD-2167A, is a top-down, single-project view of system development. Simos (1987) has noted the following:

- Software reuse is not inherently "top down."
- Reuse involves a perspective that necessarily looks beyond the development of single projects or systems.
- Reuse involves the exploitation of commonality at many levels of abstraction besides that easily captured in code.

Simos (1987) further observes:

Software reuse is not specifically addressed in the conventional top-down model, in which systems are designed via a process of modular decomposition. Hence, structured methodologies rarely include specific techniques for analyzing domains to extract maximally reusable components (though object-oriented design methods may rightly claim to improve this state of affairs to a great extent [Simos references Meyer 1987 here]). Since most applications are in fact hybrids of reuse and new design, de facto reuse does occur; yet it is often confined to ad hoc, informal contexts that fall between the cracks of the "official" methodology being followed by the project, and is dependent on developers' intuitive grasp of common functionality within the semantics of the application.

What is needed is a process model that allows for iteration between the top-down, "problem-driven" approach and a bottom-up, "parts-driven" perspective.... Such a process model would correspond more closely to the real state of practice in software development than the current model, and would at least initially have a less prescriptive, more descriptive, flavor.

Wegner (1984) states, "Life-cycle models provide a uniform framework for problem solving within which reusable methodologies and tools can be developed." He summarizes the waterfall model, the operational model, and the knowledge-based model. The idea of the operational model is to transition from an executable problem-oriented specification (serving as a rapid prototype) through a sequence of transformations to a more efficient implementation-oriented realization. Zave's PAISLey system is perhaps the best-known implementation based on this idea (Zave 1984). Wegner describes the knowledge-based model as consisting of a project database and a knowledge-based assistant. In this approach, software development is controlled by a knowledge-based activity coordinator who coordinates the access of multiple developers and users and logs the states and history of all information in the project database. Thus the computer is an active partner in program development. Wegner perceives this model as providing a framework for automating a variety of life-cycle models, including the waterfall and operational models.

Wegner considers the waterfall model to have the benefit of uniformity within a given organization—attested by Boehm's ability to devise the cost model COCOMO for use in estimating levels of effort and time schedules for software projects, with a reasonable degree of accuracy (Boehm 1981). However, Wegner expresses concern about shortcomings of the waterfall model, including its origins in manual software development activities of the 1960s, its shortcomings as to feedback, and the difficulties in performing maintenance and enhancement on low-level optimized implementations rather than on problem-oriented specifications.

Perhaps the best-known alternative to the waterfall life-cycle model is the spiral model (Boehm 1988), which recognizes that software development is not inherently sequential. The model incorporates risk analysis at each spiral phase. Boehm has not addressed reuse explicitly with the spiral model.

Simos (1987) proposes the domain-oriented software life-cycle model, which "formalizes typical patterns in the development of related series of applications and the persistence of information from one application to the next."

Raymond Yeh and his colleagues are actively pursuing software reuse in connection with the prototyping life-cycle paradigm (Yeh and Welch 1987). Hartman (1989) describes their approach, which is based on incremental interactive specification with prototyping performed at each level of development, with reuse at each level (specifications, design, code, etc.), and with maintenance performed at the specification level. Their developments include PROTO (a tool for functional prototyping) and MicroSTEP (which achieves mapping from high-level specifications to code for a specific domain). They are also engaged in U.S. Army Strategic Defense Command (SDC)–funded work to define and to implement methodology, environment, and tools to support the life-cycle model.

2.2.3 A Generic Reuse/Reusability Model

Kang (1987) suggests a refinement to the DOD-STD-2167A life cycle by identifying reuse activities applicable to each phase. He describes a generic reuse activity model developed at SEI as the base model for use in refining each phase. As noted in chapter 1, Kang defines reuse to be "an act of synthesizing a solution to a problem based on predefined solutions to subproblems." He proposes the following four steps to be performed at each phase:

1. understanding the problem and identifying a solution structure based on the predefined components;
2. reconfiguring the solution structure to improve the possibility of using predefined components available at the next phase;
3. acquiring, [assessing,] instantiating, and modifying predefined components;
4. integrating the components into the products for this phase.

Note that we have added "assessing" to Kang's third statement. While he mentions "assessing" in his discussion and his statement therefore assumes assessment is performed, we felt "assessing" should be explicitly stated for clarity. Kang offers the following comments on the four steps:

> The major tasks under the first step are to understand the problem to solve, build up the knowledge of the predefined solutions, and apply the knowledge in structuring the problem in terms of the subproblems to which solutions already exist.

> Once a solution structure is identified based on the predefined components available at a given phase, the next step is to reconfigure the solution in order to optimize reuse both at the current phase and the next phase. Doing so requires identifying experts of the next phase activity who will review the proposed solution, identifying candidate components available at the next phase, and evaluating the reusability of the candidate components. Based on the potential reuse at the next phase as well as at the current phase, an optimal solution structure is to be identified. We anticipate that the first two steps would be iterated a number of times.

> The major output from the first two steps are a solution structure and a reuse plan for the next phase. The third step includes tasks of making components identified in the solution structure ready for integration. These tasks include acquiring reusable components, modifying and/or instantiating reusable components, and developing the components that cannot be acquired or for which modification is not economic. Finally, the completed components are integrated into the product(s) required for the phase. The products are subjected to a formal review before being released to the next phase.

Kang (1987) also includes an example of the application of this generic reuse model to the software requirements phase. That discussion identifies the experts who will participate in Step 2 as domain experts. The reuse model would be applied to refine the other phases of the 2167A life cycle in much the same way. SEI is currently evaluating this approach to integrating reuse into the software process.

As the generic reuse activity model now stands, it does not deal with the contribution of reusable components to a library. The following is suggested as Step 5 (thus creating a five-step reuse/reusability model):

> 5. evaluating reusability prospects of components that must be developed and components obtained by modifying predefined components, for contribution to the set of predefined components.

This activity would include consideration of the advisability of generalizing the components for improved reusability.

It is significant to observe that this reuse/reusability model actually spans multiple projects, since the expectation is that products created within a given project will be used in other projects. Thus to be effective in software reuse, an organization must of necessity take this multi-project view of development and maintenance.

The JIAWG has described reuse activities in the framework of DOD-STD-2167A. We discuss their work in section 2.2.5.

Decisions with respect to reuse must be based on knowledge, and automation of the decision process is an important goal (e.g., Iscoe 1987). The process proposed by Kang (1987) assumes a manual decision process, based on the use of domain experts. Research is being conducted to determine better ways to perform domain analysis and to capture domain knowledge in machine-processable form. (We discuss domain analysis in section 3.1.) Kang's approach does not explicitly take into account the transformational approach to the life cycle. The goal of generating executable software from requirements has been realized so far only in very limited domains (e.g., see the reference to MicroSTEP in section 2.2.2). To the extent success is achieved, it is unnecessary to go through the life-cycle phases manually.

Dusink (1989) takes a somewhat different approach than Kang. He suggests a set of steps that go through the entire software development process, focusing on the application domain. Dusink also discusses supporting tools for his process.

Basili et al. (1989) characterize the reuse process as

1. specifying the object to be created;
2. searching the project, domain, and general databases for reuse candidates;
3. evaluating the candidates to determine which (if any) should be used;
4. modifying, if necessary, to fit specific needs;
5. integrating the reusable components;
6. validating;
7. feeding back the knowledge regarding the payoff of reuse.

2.2.4 Establishing a Process

Substantial progress is being made in devising software engineering processes that encourage reuse and reusability. While specific aspects of some approaches are presently undergoing experimental evaluation, there can be no doubt that many of the ideas are workable and can be applied with profit. Kang's generic reuse activity model, augmented with a reusability step as suggested herein, seems a very practical and workable approach to 2167A refinement. And, it would appear to be applicable as stated to any multiphase process in which phase transitions are based on manual decision making. Indeed, the same process would be required in the event of automated support to phase transitioning—the only difference being that some of the activities would be achieved by automated, knowledge-based means.

Maintenance activities were not directly addressed by Kang, but the reuse/reusability model applies equally well to software enhancement as to original development, since maintenance and original development should follow essentially the same software engineering process.

As we have previously noted, deciding on the software process (or processes) for an organization is a major decision. Consideration of Kang's model makes it clear that reuse likely can be accommodated effectively as a refinement to an organization's existing software process, perhaps lessening to some extent the impact of introducing software reuse. Whatever approach to a software engineering process is taken, software reuse and reusability should be important, integral, natural, and inescapable elements of the process.

An organization should be concerned that all aspects of the process be effective. Thus a good starting point for undertaking reuse is to assess organizational software development and maintenance practices to ensure that they are systematic and consistent, that effective tools are being employed, and that personnel are well-trained in state-of-the-practice techniques. SEI's process assessment procedure (Humphrey et al. 1987) is a well-known and accepted instrument for such assessments. Fairley et al. (1989) have suggested a reuse assessment procedure based on a questionnaire with the style of the SEI assessment questionnaire. Their "Reuse Assessment Instrument" questions are categorized by organizational issues, behavioral concerns, economic issues, methodological issues, and technological issues. They have not reached the point of assigning a maturity scale for the instrument. Examples of the organizational questions are

- Do upper level and mid-level managers understand and support the goals and objectives of software reuse? Have they issued directives or policy statements concerning reuse?
- Is the software development activity structured by domains that are amenable to reuse considerations?

Examples of questions in the methodological category are

- Are reuse considerations explicitly factored into analysis and design activities?
- Have techniques such as object-oriented development, information hiding, and data encapsulation been assessed for their reuse potential in your organization?

SEI has recently undertaken a revision of their assessment process. Perhaps more emphasis will be placed on reuse in the updated questionnaire and assessments.

The following guidelines ensue from this discussion. The last six of the guidelines are suggestive of activities that are appropriate for each phase. They summarize adaptations of the generic reuse/reusability model for the phases.

SP1: *Initiate action to establish a software engineering process (including development and maintenance) that includes reuse and reusability as important, integral, natural, and inescapable elements.*

SP2: *Augment DOD-STD-2167A with refinements that specifically support and encourage reusability and reuse (e.g., the five-step generic reuse/reusability model).*

SP3: *Emphasize effective, consistent methods for all aspects of software development and maintenance.*

SP4: *Automate activities within the software process as understanding and experience permit.*

SP5: *During the requirements determination phase, conduct the following activities:*

(1) *Make use of available requirements components as appropriate.*

(2) *Structure requirements to take advantage of available high-level designs.*

(3) *Emphasize preparation of reusable requirements components (from newly developed requirements and modified previously available requirements).*

SP6: *During the high-level-design phase, conduct the following activities:*

(1) *Make use of available high-level-design components as appropriate.*

(2) *Structure the high-level design to take advantage of available detailed designs.*

(3) *Emphasize preparation of reusable high-level-design components (from newly developed high-level designs and modified previously available high-level designs).*

SP7: *During the detailed-design phase, conduct the following activities:*

(1) *Make use of available detailed-design components as appropriate.*

(2) *Structure the detailed design to take advantage of available code modules.*

(3) *Emphasize preparation of reusable detailed-design components (from newly developed detailed designs and modified previously available detailed designs).*

SP8: *During the coding and unit-testing phase, conduct the following activities:*

(1) *Make use of available code components and test cases as appropriate.*

(2) *Emphasize preparation of reusable code components and test cases (from newly developed code/test cases and modified previously available code/test cases).*

SP9: *During integration testing, conduct the following activities:*

(1) *Make use of available test plans, test cases, and test results as appropriate.*

(2) *Emphasize preparation of reusable test plans/cases/results (from newly developed tests and modified, previously available tests).*

SP10: *Recognizing that the maintenance phase contains as subphases the software development phases, apply to maintenance the guidelines provided above for requirements, design, coding, and testing.*

2.2.5 Case Study: JIAWG Reuse-Based Process Plan

Reifer (1990) discusses approaches planned by the JIAWG to implement a software reuse program on the new aircraft programs that fall under the purview of DOD's Joint Integrated Avionics Plan for New Aircraft. The plan is to take an evolutionary rather than revolutionary approach to implement the planned software reuse program so that the JIAWG can build upon its contractor community's experience to make reuse occur in practice. It is believed that, with the advent of modern software methods, advanced tools and the Ada programming language, software reuse is now practical. The JIAWG reuse program can be viewed as the culmination of a multiyear effort aimed at replacing the ad hoc methods being used by contractors with a systematic program of reuse. It should be noted that Reifer (1990) is a draft document and that not all program offices have accepted the recommendations for implementation. However, much thought has gone into this document, and many of the recommendations will no doubt be implemented.

Management, technical, and operational approaches have been devised for the reuse program. Seven key elements have been determined for the management approach:

1. Formalize a JIAWG Reuse Office and charter it to act as the office of primary responsibility for managing software reuse.
2. Provide the JIAWG Reuse Office with the dedicated personnel and resources (time, talent, and dollars) it needs to be effective.
3. Task a reuse advocate within the JIAWG Reuse Office to provide reuse advice, direction, and focus across aircraft program offices.
4. Have a Reuse Manager within the aircraft program offices work with the JIAWG Reuse Office to implement agreed-upon reuse policies and achieve the desired degree of commonality.
5. Expand the role of the JIAWG Software Task Group's Software Reuse Subcommittee to coordinate software reuse issues within and across affected organizations.
6. Utilize the existing JIAWG's Steering Committee as an executive body to resolve conflicts and provide the software reuse program with needed oversight, management, and direction.
7. Establish a management infrastructure for the software reuse program to create the framework needed for orderly decision-making.

Technical approaches were devised to orient software engineering processes, methods and tools toward acquisition and exploitation of reusable software objects. The four key elements are

1. Interpret existing software standards (i.e., DOD-STD-2167A, etc.) in a manner that addresses reuse processes, receivables, legacy, inheritables, and deliverables.
2. Encourage the use of modern methods that cause software engineers to identify domain-specific opportunities for software reuse while they generate requirements and designs.
3. Develop specifications for Software Engineering Environment–based library tools that can be used to quickly identify and access candidate reusable software components (e.g., designs, code, tests, etc.) that meet requirements.
4. Facilitate the development and use of processes and procedures that ensure that reusable software components resident in the reuse libraries are of high quality and can be trusted by their users.

Also, operational concepts and protocols were devised to control the reuse management and technical processes. These controls are based on implementation of a number of contractual and legal initiatives, changes in infrastructure and the efficient use of a distributed software reuse library system.

Details are provided in Reifer (1990) for the management, technical, and operational approaches. We will limit further discussion here to the structuring of reuse processes for compatibility with DOD-STD-2167A. Reifer provides details for each 2167A phase; Inputs, Process, and Outputs are shown for each phase. For Inputs, References are shown; for Process, Process Controls are shown; and for Outputs, Reviews are shown.

For example, consider the Systems Requirements Analysis Phase.

INPUTS   Receivables: solicitations and studies
          Inheritables: infrastructure
          References: DOD-STD-2167A, DOD-STD-2168 (Defense System Software Quality Program), MIL-STD-1521B (Technical Reviews and Audits for Systems, Equipments, and Computer Programs)

PROCESS   Perform domain analysis
          Identify reuse opportunities
          Conduct reuse analysis
          Perform cost/benefit analysis
          Process controls: checklists, gating criteria, methodology rules, reuse reviews

OUTPUTS   Deliverables: System Specification, Software Development Plan, with reuse aspects

Reviews: System Requirements Review, Proposal Review

As a final example, we provide the following details for Systems Design Phase.

INPUTS   Receivables: System specification
Inheritables: Generic plans, processes, standards, guides, etc.
References: DOD-STD-2167A, DOD-STD-2168, MIL-STD-1521B

PROCESS Develop reuse plans
Identify potential reusable components
Perform make/buy analysis
Initiate mining efforts
Form reuse working group
Acquire/activate reuse library
Process Controls: checklists, gating criteria, methodology rules, reuse reviews

OUTPUTS Deliverables: system specification, system design document, etc. (as required by 2167A)
Reviews: System Design Review

In addition to such details for each phase, the document gives flow-diagram scenarios for acquisition/development, operation, and population of libraries.

The extensive, detailed planning for this reuse program are impressive. It will be instructive to follow the progress of the program as it proceeds.

2.3 References

AdaIC (Ada Information Clearing House). June 1990. *Ada Information Clearinghouse Newsletter.* 8(2).

Aharonian, G. July 1989. "Working paper." In *Proceedings of the Reuse in Practice Workshop*, ed. J. Baldo and C. Braun. Software Engineering Institute, Pittsburgh, Penn.

Baker, B., and A. Deeds. July 1989. "Industrial Policy and Software Reuse: A Systems Approach." In *Proceedings of the Reuse in Practice Workshop*, ed. J. Baldo and C. Braun. Software Engineering Institute, Pittsburgh, Penn.

Barnes, B., T. Durek, J. Gaffney, and A. Pyster. October 1987. "A Framework and Economic Foundation for Software Reuse." In *Proceedings of the Workshop on Software Reuse*, ed. G. Booch and L. Williams. Rocky Mountain Inst. of Software Engineering, SEI, MCC, Software Productivity Consortium, Boulder, Colo.

Basili, V. R., H. D. Rombach, J. Bailey, A. Delis, and F. Farhat. March 1989. "Ada Reuse Metrics." In *Guidelines Document for Ada Reuse and Metrics (Draft)*, ed. P. A. Lesslie, R. O. Chester, and M. F. Theofanos, 11–29. K/DSRD-54, Martin Marietta Energy Systems, Inc., Oak Ridge, Tenn., under contract to U.S. Army, AIRMICS.

Belady, L.A. 1989. "Foreword." In *Software Reusability, Vol. I, Concepts and Models*, ed. T. J. Biggerstaff and A. J. Perlis, vii–viii. ACM Press, Addison-Wesley, Reading, Mass.

Biggerstaff, T. J., and A. J. Perlis, ed. 1989a. *Software Reusability. Concepts and Models*, vol. I, ACM Press, Addison-Wesley, Reading, Mass.

Biggerstaff, T. J., and A. J. Perlis, ed. 1989b. *Software Reusability. Applications and Experience*, vol. II, ACM Press, Addison-Wesley, Reading, Mass.

Boehm, B. W. 1981. *Software Engineering Economics*. Prentice-Hall, Englewood Cliffs, NJ.

Boehm, B. W. May 1988. "A Spiral Model of Software Development and Enhancement." *Computer* 21(5), 61–72.

Bollinger, T. B. and S. L. Pfleeger. March 1990. "The Economics of Reuse: Issues and Alternatives." In *Proceedings of the Eighth Annual National Conference on Ada Technology*, 436–47. Atlanta, GA.

Burton, B. A., R. W. Aragon, S. A. Bailey, K. D. Koehler, and L. A. Mayes. July 1987. "The Reusable Software Library." *IEEE Software* 4(4), 25–33.

Cavaliere, M. J. 1983. "Reusable Code at the Hartford Insurance Group." In *Proceedings of the Workshop on Reusability in Programming*. Newport, R.I.

Curtis, B. 1989. "Cognitive Issues in Reusing Software Artifacts." In *Software Reusability. Applications and Experience*, vol. II, Biggerstaff, T. J., and A. J. Perlis, 269-87. ACM Press, Addison-Wesley, Reading, Mass.

Dusink, E. M. July 1989. "Towards a Design Philosophy for Reuse." In *Proceedings of the Reuse in Practice Workshop*, ed. J. Baldo and C. Braun. Software Engineering Institute, Pittsburgh, Penn.

Fairley, R., S. L. Pfleeger, T. Bollinger, A. Davis, A. J. Incorvaia, and B. Springsteen. 1989. *Final Report: Incentives for Reuse of Ada Components, vols. 1 through 5*. George Mason University, Fairfax, Va.

Hall, P. A. V. January 1987. "Software Components and Reuse– Getting More Out of Your Code." *Information and Software Technology* 29(1), 38–43.

Hartman, D. February 1989. "Rapid Prototyping Using Reuse." In *Reuse and the Software Revolution Symposium*. Falcon Air Force Base, Colo.

Humphrey, W. S. June 1989. "The Software Engineering Process: Definition and Scope." *Software Engineering Notes* 14(4), 82–83.

Humphrey, W. S., W. L. Sweet, R. K. Edwards, G. R. Lacrois, M. F. Ownes, and H. P. Schultz. September 1987. "A Method for Assessing the Software Engineering Capability of Contractors," CMU/SEI-87-TR-23, Software Engineering Institute, Pittsburgh.

Iscoe, N. October 1987. "A Knowledge Based and Object-Oriented Approach to Reusability Within Application Domains." In *Proceedings of the Workshop on Software Reuse*, ed. G. Booch and L. Williams. Rocky Mountain Inst. of Software Engineering, SEI, MCC, Software Productivity Consortium, Boulder, Colo.

Joiner, H. F. July 1989. "Position Paper on Software Reuse." In *Proceedings of the Reuse in Practice Workshop*, ed. J. Baldo and C. Braun. Software Engineering Institute, Pittsburgh, Penn.

Kang, K. C. October 1987. "A Reuse-Based Software Development Methodology." In *Proceedings of the Workshop on Software Reuse*, ed. G. Booch and L. Williams. Rocky Mountain Inst. of Software Engineering, SEI, MCC, Software Productivity Consortium, Boulder, Colo.

Meyer, B. March 1987. "Reusability: The Case for Object-Oriented Design." *IEEE Software* 4(2), 50–64.

Myers, W. July 1990. "'We Want to Write Less Code,' Asserts Symposium Keynoter." *Computer* 23(7), 117-118.

Reifer, D. J. June 1990. "Joint Integrated Avionics Working Group Reusable Software Program Operational Concept Document (OCD)" (Draft). RCI-TR-075B, Reifer Consultants, Inc. (Torrance, CA).

Simos, M. A. October 1987. "The Domain-Oriented Software Life Cycle: Towards an Extended Process Model for Reusability." In *Proceedings of the Workshop on Software Reuse*, ed. G. Booch and L. Williams. Rocky Mountain Inst. of Software Engineering, SEI, MCC, Software Productivity Consortium, Boulder, Colo.

Taylor, C. July 1989. "Software Reuse." In *Proceedings of the Reuse in Practice Workshop*, ed. J. Baldo and C. Braun. Software Engineering Institute, Pittsburgh, Penn.

Tracz, W. April 1990. "Where Does Reuse Start?" *ACM Software Eng. Notes* 15(2), 42-46.

Tully, C., ed. June 1989. "Proceedings of the 4th International Software Process Workshop, Devon UK, May, 1988." *Software Engineering Notes* 14(4), 82–83.

Wald, E. 1986. *STARS Reusability Guidebook, V4.0* (Draft). U.S. Department of Defense, STARS.

Wegner, P. July 1984. "Capital-Intensive Software Technology." *IEEE Software* 1(3).

Yeh, R. T., and T. A. Welch. October 1987. "Software Evolution: Forging a Paradigm." In *Proceedings of The 1987 Fall Joint Computer Conference*, 10–12. Dallas.

Zave, P. February 1984. "The Operational Versus the Conventional Approach to Life Cycle Development." *ACM Communications* 27(2).

Technical Guidelines

In this chapter we consider technical issues of software reuse. Guidelines and methods are provided for domain analysis; for preparation of reusable components—including requirements, designs, and code; and for reuse of available components—including repository considerations. Case studies concerning domain analysis, reusable designs, reusable code, and a library system for software reuse are also provided.

3.1 Domain Analysis

3.1.1 Overview

Careful needs assessments must be made before developing components for reuse. Considerably higher development costs for reusable component development than for single-use components must be taken into consideration. This may be because of the form the reusable software takes (generic, parameterized, application generator, etc.) and the rigor necessary in testing it.

Two categories of software components seem to be good candidates for reuse: horizontally reusable and vertically reusable components. Horizontal reuse refers to reuse across a broad range of application areas such as data structures, sorting algorithms, and user-interface mechanisms; vertical reuse refers to components within a given application area that can be reused in similar applications within the same problem domain (Tracz 1987a). Horizontal reuse has, no doubt, been more studied to date (Booch 1987a), and it likely has been employed much more frequently than vertical reuse. The main reasons for this are that horizontal reuse is better understood and easier to achieve. On the other hand, the greatest potential leverage can come from vertical reuse—by intensive reuse of carefully crafted solutions to problems within an application domain. The CAMP project (McNicholl et al. 1986) is an example of vertical reuse. In all six successful reuse projects examined by Fairley et al. (1989), reuse was practiced in narrow, well-defined domains.

In order to achieve vertical reuse, a domain analysis is required. Prieto-Diaz (1990) defines domain analysis as "a process by which information used in developing software systems is identified, captured, and organized with the purpose of making it reusable when creating new systems." He states that "domain analysis deals with the development and evolution of an information infrastructure to support reuse." The information generated during software development spans the entire range of activities, including requirements, designs, and source code, and also includes code documentation, history of design decisions, testing plans, and user manuals. An objective of domain analysis is to provide all such information in convenient forms for use in making reuse decisions. The source code contains no information about the context and decisions underlying the code; thus it is important to provide this information along with the source code.

Even more leverage is gained from reuse if domain analysis can derive common architectures, generic models, or specialized languages that characterize software in a specific problem area. In order to determine such architectures or languages, features common to a domain of applications must be identified, objects and operations that characterize these features must be selected and abstracted, and procedures must be created that automate the operations. Prieto-Diaz states that this intelligence-intensive activity typically results after several of the "same kind" systems have been constructed. Then the decision is made to "isolate, encapsulate, and standardize certain recurring operations. This is the very process of domain analysis: identifying and structuring information for reusability" (Prieto-Diaz 1990).

At present, domain analysis is a slow, unstructured learning process. Knowledge of a domain is gained over time until sufficient experience and understanding lead to a threshold at which an abstraction can be synthesized and made available for reuse. Prieto-Diaz emphasizes the need to develop formal approaches to domain analysis, including ways to extract, organize, represent, manipulate, and understand reusable information; to formalize the domain analysis process; and to develop technologies and tools to support it. Section 3.1.2 reports on a project underway at SEI that is investigating means to improve domain analysis activities and products.

Kang (1989) reports on domain analysis work at SEI. He describes domain analysis as follows:

> Domain analysis is a phase in the software life cycle where a domain model, which describes the common functions, data and relationships of a family of systems in the domain, a dictionary, which defines the terminologies used in the domain, and a software architecture, which describes the packaging,

control, and interfaces, are produced. The information necessary to produce a domain model, a dictionary, and an architecture is gathered, organized, and represented during the
domain analysis.

Domain analysis is related to requirements analysis but it is
performed in a much broader scope and generates different
results. It encompasses a family of systems in a domain, pro-
duces a domain model with parameterization to accommodate
the differences, and defines a standard architecture based on
which software components can be developed and integrated.
A domain model and an associated dictionary represent the
domain knowledge, and an architecture represents the framework for developing reusable components and for synthesizing systems from the reusable components. An ideal domain
model and architecture would be applicable throughout the
life-cycle from requirements analysis through maintenance.

In the first paragraph of the quote above from Kang, he refers to
domain analysis as a life-cycle phase. Domain analysis is, however,
an activity from which multiple software development projects are
expected to benefit. Thus we should not expect that domain analysis
would be conducted as a part of each software development project,
if results of a previous effort are available.

Kang (1989) also answers the question, "Why do we need to do
domain analysis?"

As the areas to which computers are applied become larger,
one of the problems faced by the industry is that it is often difficult to find software engineers who have the required
application domain knowledge. Reuse of application domain
knowledge is becoming an important issue in software engineering. The purpose of domain analysis is to gather and
represent application domain knowledge in a model and to
develop an architecture that shows how the problems in a
domain are addressed in software systems. A domain model
unifies and consolidates the domain knowledge which may be
reused in subsequent developments.

More and more organizations consider software as an asset
that can provide an important edge in business competition.
Therefore, identifying areas that will maximize the return on
software investment is an activity that encompasses both business planning and software engineering. The business planning activity identifies future products, and the domain analysis activity identifies the product commonality and potential

software assets. The information on the software assets can be fed back to future business planning. Also, the product commonality information enables large-grain reuse across the products.

The productivity and quality improvement from reusing components built for the purpose of reuse is much greater than that from components developed without reuse in mind. However, in order to build reusable components, the contexts in which the reusable components will be used must be understood and the reusable components must be designed to accommodate the contextual differences. A domain model and an architecture define the contexts for developing reusable components.

Kang (1989) also briefly summarizes an approach to domain analysis and provides the following summary of the paper:

Domain analysis is an activity to produce a domain model, a dictionary of terminologies used in a domain, and a software architecture for a family of systems. The outputs from the domain analysis

- facilitate reuse of domain knowledge in systems development,
- define a context in which reusable components can be developed and the reusability of candidate components can be ascertained,
- provide a model for classifying, storing, and retrieving software components,
- provide a framework for tooling and systems synthesis from the reusable components,
- allow large-grain reuse across products, and
- can be used to identify software assets.

Based on our experience with a domain analysis (called features analysis in this project) and the potential benefits from it, we believe that domain analysis should be a standard activity in the software development life cycle.

Lee and Rissman (1989) describe their work at SEI in determining domain-specific software architectures.

Prieto-Diaz (1990) states that Neighbors coined the term "domain analysis" (Neighbors 1981), and that the CAMP Project was the first recorded experience in domain analysis (CAMP 1987). He discussed McCain's efforts to describe a process for domain analysis (McCain

1985), including initially conducting a market analysis to assess the feasibility of a product, and then (1) identifying reusable entities, (2) abstracting or generalizing, and (3) classifying and cataloging for further reuse. Prieto-Diaz reports that this product-oriented paradigm has been tested successfully in several projects at IBM Federal Systems.

Prieto-Diaz discusses his earlier work resulting in a procedural model for domain analysis (Prieto-Diaz 1987), based on the use of a series of data-flow diagrams. His proposed outputs include a domain model, domain taxonomy, domain language, domain standards, and reusable components. A project at GTE Laboratories is currently underway to test these approaches. He also summarizes Cleaveland's work relating to application generators, and the relationship of this work to domain analysis (Cleveland 1988), and Arango's efforts toward integrating domain analysis into the software development process of a self-improving (learning) system for reuse (Arango 1988).

Prieto-Diaz (1990) summarizes the (phi)NIX project at Schlumberger-Doll (Barstow 1985), which is an example of a domain-specific automatic programming system pertaining to oil-well logging. The system separates domain knowledge from programming knowledge. Prieto-Diaz also summarizes domain analysis relationships to library science, expert systems, and object-oriented software development.

Cohen (1989) summarizes a domain analysis methodology in eight steps citing (Prieto-Diaz 1987) as the source for the methodology. He also shows the steps in flow-diagram form. The steps are

1. Select specific functions/objects.
2. Abstract functions/objects.
3. Define taxonomy.
4. Identify common features.
5. Identify specific relationships.
6. Abstract the relationships.
7. Derive a functional model.
8. Define a domain language.

A domain language could take one of many possible forms: a conventional language, a knowledge-based system, an object-oriented system, or another available formalism.

Prieto-Diaz (1987) comments on the need to define a domain boundary—i.e., where one domain ends and another begins. Also, he views the domain-specific language, produced in Step 8 above, as encapsulated in a formal language and serving as a specification language for the construction of systems in the domain. He characterizes this as the "reuse of analysis of information," and states the opinion that this "is the most powerful sort of reuse."

Prieto-Diaz (1987) briefly summarizes the domain analysis approaches used by Raytheon (in the work reported by Lanergan and Grasso 1984) and by McDonnell Douglas in the CAMP work (McNicholl et al. 1986). Palmer (1989) of McDonnell Douglas provides the following observations from the CAMP work:

> CAMP-1 began with a domain analysis that involved the missile operational flight software from a set of ten missiles. From this analysis, we identified approximately 250 common parts and developed a taxonomy with which to categorize those parts. We assumed (and were proved correct) that we would identify additional parts once we actually began development of the common parts. Our final part count at the end of CAMP-2 was 454.

> There are as yet no widely accepted or established techniques for performing a domain analysis, but a number of issues have been identified. One factor that is critical is the selection of an adequate domain representation set upon which to base the analysis. Practical constraints prevent the examination of all applications within a domain, thus, it is important that the sample set include applications that are truly representative of the domain as it has been defined.

Neighbors (1987) reports on the deliberations of the Domain Analysis Working Group at the Workshop on Software Reuse held in October 1987. The report states that "given a domain analysis, an organization should be able to (1) use the domain model to check the specifications and requirements for a new required system in the domain; (2) educate new people in the organization providing them with the general structure and operation of systems in the domain; and (3) derive operational systems directly from the statement of the system in domain specific terms."

The working group undertook the domain analysis of library management systems as a practical problem, with the same individuals serving as both domain experts and domain analysts. Neighbors (1987) describes the group's activities in some detail and concludes by giving the following "Basic Domain Analysis Process."

1. Establish the domain subject area.
2. Collect the domain experts.
3. Establish the depth of analysis (i.e., whether to analyze subdomains).

4. Establish the width of analysis (i.e., determine the boundary of the domain—"Is this function required by most of the systems built in this domain?").
5. Define the specific domain objects, operations, relationships, and constraints.
6. Hand test the domain by attempting a description of a specific system in the domain.
7. Package the domain for constructive reusability by expressing it in a form for a transformational refinement tool such as Draco.

The working group members used various analysis representations, including data-flow diagrams, entity-relationship diagrams, semantic nets, object diagrams, and class hierarchies with inheritance. They concluded that usually only one each from the object hierarchy, data flow, and control flow representations would be needed.

Hutchinson and Hindley (1988) report on their work in developing a domain analysis method. Their goals were

- to discover the functions that underwrite reusability,
- to focus the domain specialist's attention on reuse,
- to help the domain specialist ascertain reuse parameters,
- to discover how to redesign existing components for reuse,
- to organize a domain for reuse.

The domain analysis was done by a reuse analyst with the assistance of a domain specialist—an individual with an excellent understanding of the problem domain. The researchers developed structured domain analysis techniques based on questions devised to assess a software component's reusability. The domain on which they based their experimentation was a simulation of the utility systems management system of the Experimental Aircraft Programme (EAP) in the United Kingdom. The subdomains they considered were propulsion, fuel management, and undercarriage. The propulsion subdomain was considered for reuse because the controlled hardware (the engines) would not change significantly between the EAP implementation and the next project; fuel management was chosen because the domain appeared to contain a lot of functional duplication within the requirements definition. Undercarriage was chosen because much of its operation would not change on future implementations.

The reuse analyst decided on three levels of reuse to clarify the domain: the initial level pertained to reuse of the whole system, the next level to reuse of subsystems, and the final level to functions at the requirements level and to components at the design and code levels. The reuse analyst presented 12 questions to the domain specialist, based on the assumption that domain-specific knowledge can isolate reusable components. The questions sought to elicit identification of reuse attributes and reusable components in an understandable manner. The questions were as follows:

- Is component functionality required on future implementations?
- How common is the component's function within the domain?
- Is there duplication of the component's function within the domain?
- Is the component hardware-dependent?
- Does the hardware remain unchanged between implementations?
- Can the hardware specifics be removed to another component?
- Is the design optimized enough for the next implementation?
- Can we parameterize a nonreusable component so that it becomes reusable?
- Is the component reusable in many implementations with only minor changes?
- Is reuse through modification feasible?
- Can a nonreusable component be decomposed to yield reusable components?
- How valid is component decomposition for reuse?

The authors observe that reuse proved to be practical, even in the hardware-dependent areas being analyzed. They assessed the requirements functions as potentially 75 percent reusable for the next implementation and indicated that reuse could be equally high for code designed for reuse from these requirements.

Tracz (1987a) also goes through an example of domain analysis, and the subsequent reusable software design, based on his use of both parameterization and application generators. His general approach to software composition is summarized in section 3.3.5.

Prieto-Diaz (1990) depicts the process of domain analysis by means of an SADT context diagram (figure 1), which shows the inputs, outputs, controls, and mechanisms of domain analysis. Input information is obtained from existing systems and includes source code, documentation, designs, user manuals, and test plans. Also domain knowledge is input, along with requirements for current and future systems. The personnel involved perform their work with the guidance of domain analysis methods and management procedures. As the figure shows, feedback from the knowledge gained from the resulting output and its application to other systems can help refine the process of domain analysis. The domain analyst coordinates the analysis

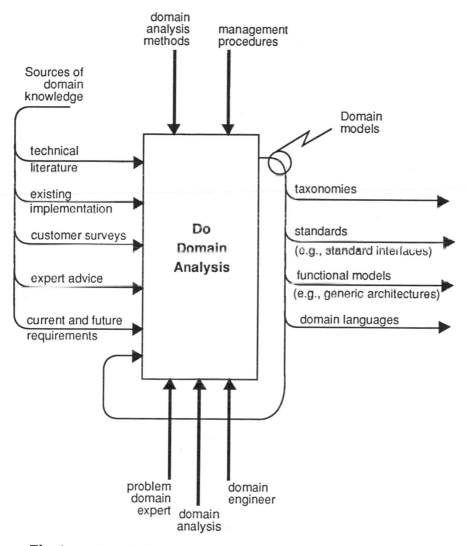

Fig. 1. SADT CONTEXT VIEW OF DOMAIN ANALYSIS (PRIETO-DIAZ 1990).

process. The domain expert supports the input (acquisition) phase, and the domain engineer supports the output (encapsulation) phase. The "standards" output may include software development methods and procedures, coding standards, management policies, and library maintenance procedures.

Figure 2 depicts the integration of domain analysis into the software development process (the "reuse infrastructure"). Domain models (of varying forms) support and control the phases of software development, guiding the selection and integration of reusable resources. Reuse data is collected and fed back to domain analysis, for use in refining the models and for updating the library. Prieto-Diaz mentions that the waterfall development model could be replaced by others, such as rapid prototyping.

While Prieto-Diaz does not discuss the maintenance process, it must also be supported by such an infrastructure. The feasibility of such is evident when it is considered that the maintenance process consists of activities that characterize the development phases (requirements determination, design, coding and unit testing, integration, and system testing).

The personnel identified by Prieto-Diaz as necessary for this process (shown in figure 2) are the librarian (who provides a library system and services to make assets available for reuse), the asset manager (who ensures compliance with asset standards), and the reuse manager (who coordinates the overall reuse effort, and supports reuse data collection).

Prieto-Diaz (1990) discusses several issues in domain analysis research. Among these are knowledge representation—how to represent domain knowledge so that it is easily understood by humans and also machine processable. He mentions such approaches as entity-relationship (E-R) diagrams, predicate logic, semantic nets, production rules, and frames. These approaches support such artificial intelligence–related functions as learning and inference. Also, database systems can offer important support to knowledge representation. Hypertext is an increasingly-important tool for interrelating components of information in an understandable way.

Knowledge acquisition is another research issue discussed by Prieto-Diaz. He states that meta-knowledge (the procedural knowledge on how to use declarative knowledge) is crucial to domain analysis, but the expert systems community considers meta-knowledge to be the hardest kind of knowledge to elicit from experts. He mentions the COMPASS project at GTE Laboratories, which involved a significant effort to elicit, capture, and encapsulate meta-knowledge about diagnostic heuristics for use in digital switch maintenance.

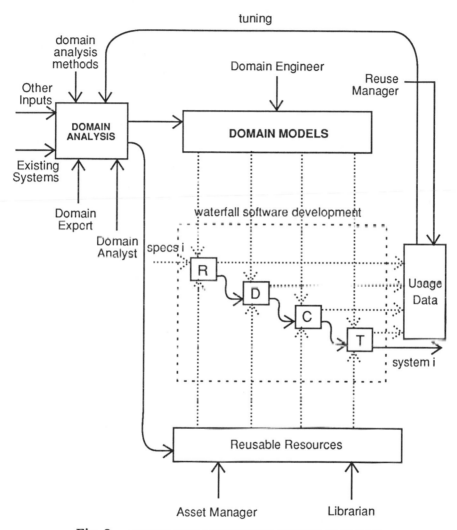

Fig. 2. A REUSE INFRASTRUCTURE (PRIETO-DIAZ 1990).

Another research issue mentioned by Prieto-Diaz (1990) is the feedback mechanism required to refine a software development model based on reuse. He cites work by Basili and Rombach (1988) at the University of Maryland who use an experimental prototype environment, TAME (Tailoring a Measurement Environment), to support reuse by explicitly modeling learning, reuse, and feedback activities. An "experience base" records software development experience and promotes "tailoring" and "generalizing" cycles on project-specific, domain-specific, and domain-independent information.

Prieto-Diaz summarizes by observing that the nature of the domain analysis process requires a variety of multidisciplinary approaches ranging from knowledge acquisition and representation, to management and methodologies, to cultural and social questions.

Hess et al. (1990) is an extensive annotated bibliography of domain analysis literature that can be a valuable source document. The document summarizes 86 references, as follows:

1. a set of full document citations and annotations
2. a table showing how the references fit within the following classification:
   (a) information gathering
   (b) domain analysis methodology
   (c) tools and environment support
   (d) representation (domain models and domain architectures)
   (e) application domains
   (f) management issues
3. an alphabetical cross reference by author's name
4. a chronological ordering by year of publication
5. an alphabetical cross reference by project and sponsor names
6. an alphabetical index listing the citation key and the page number where the full citation may be found

Some experienced software engineers make the observation that domain analysis activities have much in common with system engineering. Certainly if system engineering analyses already exist (for example, in large DOD programs) that provide information on commonality, as much benefit should be derived from the analyses as practical.

We conclude this section by suggesting the following guidelines.

DA1: *Select domain(s) carefully for analysis, based on the maturity and stability of the organization's activities within each domain and on the planned emphasis the domain is to receive.*

DA2: *Determine and apply a systematic approach to domain analysis, yielding a domain model, a set of domain terminology, and a domain architecture.*

DA3: *Use domain analysis results as a basis for classifying, storing, and retrieving reusable components.*

DA4: *Use domain analysis results as a basis for decisions about the advisability of investing in specific instances of reusable software.*

DA5: *Use domain analysis results to help understand how existing domain-specific reusable software may be applied.*

DA6: *Take advantage of existing system engineering analyses that identify commonality.*

3.1.2 Case Study: The Domain Analysis Project at Software Engineering Institute (SEI)

This section provides an overview of the work of the SEI Domain Analysis, as documented by SEI (1990). At the time of the briefing (June 1990) SEI had not yet issued a technical report. Thus the information provided in this section should be understood to be preliminary, but it can nonetheless be beneficial in gaining insights into the still immature endeavor of domain analysis.

The Domain Analysis Project at SEI has the following objectives:

- To develop domain analysis products that support implementation of new applications. This includes
  - understanding the domain,
  - supporting user-developer communication, and
  - providing reuse requirements.
- To establish domain analysis methods to produce these products.

This project is underway at SEI and is scheduled for completion in March 1991. The phased approach has consisted of a feasibility phase for developing and testing methods, a development phase for applying methods to the new domain, and a transition phase for conveying results to customers.

Various personnel play roles relative to domain analysis methods. The sources are end users of systems in the domain, and domain experts provide information about systems in the domain. The producer is the domain analyst who gathers information and performs analysis. The consumers for methods are requirements analysts who specify systems in the domain, software engineers who design new systems in the domain, and the end users of systems in the domain.

In the approach of this project, the domain analysis methodology structure consists of context analysis, domain modeling, and architecture modeling. The overall objective of domain analysis is to capture commonalities and differences of systems in the domain and to represent the information in exploitable form. Commonalities are captured by means of abstraction mechanisms: aggregation/decomposition, generalization/specialization, and parameterization. Context analysis involves scoping the domain and analyzing the variability of external conditions; domain modeling consists of analyzing and modeling domain problems. Architecture modeling involves analysis and modeling of application architectures for the domain problems.

Context analysis results in a context model that consists of a structure diagram showing how the domain is placed relative to other domains and a top-level, data-flow diagram ("context diagram") showing external entities and data flows between the domain and the external entities.

Domain modeling results are recorded by means of entity-relationship models, features models, functional models (using finite-state machines and data-flow diagrams), and a domain terminology dictionary. The entity-relationship models are made up of a combination of Chen's entity-relationship model notation, semantic data models (is-a, consists-of), and constraints. Features models (i.e., features diagrams) give the end-user's perspective of the capabilities (mandatory, optional, and alternative) of applications in a domain, by means of AND/OR graphs. Compatibility between features is defined as composition rules, stated textually. Capabilities of an application are defined as an instantiation of the features model.

Architecture modeling is achieved by means of a process interaction model (using the DARTS methodology), and module structure charts. Work on this aspect of the methodology is currently underway.

The project has conducted a successful domain analysis of the domain of window managers, employing the methodology summarized above. Their domain information sources were four domain experts, user experience with eight different window systems, and domain literature (books, articles, manuals, surveys, product evaluations). As to enumerated domain features, the sources were as follows: 41 percent direct experience, 38 percent domain experts, 13 percent system documentation, and 8 percent general knowledge.

The structure diagram of window systems is shown as a cube depicting the relationship of window systems to executing applications and to device driver, server, protocol, library, toolkit, and window manager applications. In addition to the structure diagram, the context model consists of a context diagram (i.e., high-level data-flow diagram) showing the data flowing between the window manager and the input manager, process manager, and screen manager as well as constraints and parameters.

The window manager dictionary has 250 entries, and many synonyms. The briefing charts (SEI 1990) show example feature diagrams for the MOVE operation, some feature composition rules (e.g., zapEffect requires eraseAfter), and a system feature catalogue example for MOVE.

The Project is using an automated tool, StateMate, to support the process of features selection and instantiation. The approach is based on storing features in a Prolog fact base. The tool supports the definition of existing or proposed systems by means of sets of features. The tool enforces the composition rules, and performs consistency and completeness checks.

The functional model for the window managers domain analysis was based on Statecharts and Activitycharts. Commonalities are captured by common states and transitions in Statecharts; common activities and data flows for input and output are depicted by Activitycharts. Differences are represented by conditions on control flow in Statecharts and by optional data flows in Activitycharts. Statecharts are decomposed by means of separate charts, and textual descriptions are used to link states to activities and to show optional data flows. The Project summarizes the strengths of Statemate in this application by saying that it is a good analysis tool and that it supports parameterization. The weaknesses they noted are that it is not scalable without tailoring and transitions and conditionals hide commonality. It is also difficult to transition.

The project offers the following observations among others:

- Proper domain scoping is critical to success.
- The feature model is central. It parameterizes all the other models.
- Real/proposed systems can be described by sets of feature values.
- There is a need for automated representation.
- Current tools will not all scale.
- The approach should be to scope along architectural, not logical, boundaries.
- Model representations may be domain-specific.
- There is no global domain expert—only local experts.
- Domains analyzed should be stable.

- Lessons learned should be recorded.

The project is undertaking domain analysis of a DOD activity. They will be providing their final report on that work and on the domain analysis methodology in March 1991.

3.2 Creating Reusable Components

3.2.1 Spanning the Life Cycle

The goal of practitioners of software reuse should be to make use of existing knowledge and software artifacts throughout the software life cycle (wide-spectrum reuse), with the expectation that the earlier the reuse occurs in the life cycle, the greater should be the payoff. Code reuse is better understood and more prevalent by far than other levels of reuse, but reuse of other kinds of software components is accelerating.

As we have previously noted, there are additional costs when preparing software components for reuse because of the necessary effort to generalize the components, to conduct extra testing, to document the components, and to classify and store them for reuse. Tracz (1990) rightly emphasizes the point that, while it is desirable to capitalize on existing software resources and expertise, an organization must develop a "business case" to justify the additional cost of developing reusable software. Thus it is important that a careful assessment be made of the likely payoff of such extra costs. This decision process is inherent in step 5 of the suggested reuse/reusability model in section 2.2.3.

As to what kinds of products to reuse, Tracz (1990) discusses code, designs, specification, problem definition, test cases and documentation. Higher-granularity code components give a larger "win" in productivity, suggesting the use of larger code components such as software packages, modules, or classes. Biggerstaff and Perlis (1989a) discuss the difficulties in achieving a good balance in the size of code components. Since code components have a high degree of specificity, the most highly reusable components tend to be small. However, so much work is required to bind such components into a whole system, that the cost to build the superstructure is much greater than the savings afforded by reusing small components. On the other hand, while it might appear that large code components would remove the difficulties, their specificity makes them unlikely to be usable without modification in satisfying any given requirement; and their greater size compounds the problem of understanding and modifying them for use. Biggerstaff and Perlis believe that, in order to realize the full potential for reuse, "Very Large Scale Reuse" (VLSR) must be achieved—requiring representations that permit precise descriptions of large-grain component structures, while leaving many small, relatively unimportant details uncommitted until the time of use. Their idea is that such representations should include much more than source code; examples given are design structures, domain knowledge, and design decisions.

As Tracz (1990) points out, software reuse generally ends by using code, but it may start with products of higher levels of abstraction, depending on (1) how much effort an organization is willing to invest in preparing products for reuse, (2) how effectively higher-abstraction products can be linked to available implementations, (3) how effectively implementations are generalized, and (4) how effectively the software process supports software reuse.

Tracz discusses some issues of software reuse relating to the software development process. He summarizes by saying that the ability to reuse software at different life cycle phases depends upon (1) modifying the development process to identify opportunities for reuse, and (2) modifying or extending the software life cycle to identify components to make reusable. He emphasizes that software reuse is a good example of software engineering discipline.

Tracz comments that reuse at design time involves both the bottom-up approach of reuse, and (usually) the top-down design approach. He states that an object-oriented design approach can help match a design to implementations, but that parameterization is the key to controlling the process. In all phases, reuse can be better accommodated by identifying early in the life cycle what pertinent components are available for reuse; then specification trade-offs can be made, and designs can be tailored, to leverage from the existing software base.

Tracz comments on his view that domain analysis is a generalization of requirements analysis—i.e., requirements of a generic application are quantified over a domain. (Domain analysis is discussed in section 3.1.) Domain analysis can thus be viewed as a new life-cycle phase that has been devised to support reuse. (Of course, each software development project need not conduct domain analysis, if results of a previous effort are available.)

Tracz mentions that code review time and design review time both provide opportunities to reuse software, and to assess the reuse potential of software. Viewing reuse from the standpoint of individual projects, he notes that project start-up is a good time to define a software process that accommodates reuse. Reusable software libraries can be set up, and standards and tools developed. He mentions a successful reuse project in which reuse started at the beginning of the project. The project was a Computer Integrated Manufacturing effort in which 350K lines of Ada source code were developed. A Project Reuse Lead was assigned to sit in on all design and specification reviews to identify commonality between subsystems and to support the communication and application of reuse technology. Because of reuse, the size and development effort of the project was reduced by more than 20 percent.

Another time to consider reuse is at the end of a project, when the participants can record how to modify the system for future reuse. Tracz mentions an example of this at General Dynamics; when a project was completed, and before the personnel were assigned to other projects, "they locked everyone up in a room and wouldn't let them out until they developed an archetype of the system"—i.e., recorded how and what to modify for future reuse.

While Tracz does not discuss reuse relative to software maintenance, reuse should be considered to be just as important in modifying and upgrading software as in development of new software. In fact, the same kinds of products can be reused in maintenance as in new development, and the same personnel issues occur. While the process is certainly different for maintenance, it in fact subsumes all the phases of software development. Considering that maintenance costs overwhelm development costs in the case of many large systems, reuse could provide an even greater return during maintenance.

Lubars (1987) of MCC discusses the potential reuse of many kinds of software components, including domain-related knowledge, requirements, abstract designs, abstract algorithms, design and program transformations, and code. Also important for reuse are test plans, test cases, and test results. Research is being conducted to generate code from requirements through automatic transformations (e.g., Baxter 1987). Some success has been achieved in very narrow domains (e.g., Hartman 1989), yet in the foreseeable future manual transformations will be necessary in moving from phase to phase in the software life cycle. The greatest occurrence of high-level reuse is probably in "personnel reuse"—when individuals who previously have analyzed requirements for similar systems apply their retained insights and approaches.

A great deal of "implicit" reuse takes place when products are reused. For example, when a code module is reused, a design is being reused, and to some extent requirements are being reused. Thus benefit is derived by not having to repeat preceding activities. In section 3.2.2.1 we will see that so-called "generators" actually incorporate (and thus reuse) a very great deal of requirements and design information.

A code component retained "in isolation" in a reuse library is likely to be of little value. Thus it is extremely important that design and requirements associated with code modules be retained, along with test plans, test cases, test results, prototypes (perhaps), and other related life-cycle products. The associated set of components can be useful in many ways. For example, determining a match (or near match) with reusable requirements may lead to reuse of the associated design and code, or at least to reuse of the high-level design. Clearly, the high-level design should be easier to understand and adapt than the associated code would be. And, the high-level and detailed designs should be very valuable in understanding code.

Since, for now, reusable components will be reused manually within the software process, the organization of the library and the means for searching and retrieving related sets of candidate components and for understanding and adapting components are very important considerations. In section 3.2.5 we consider issues of classifying and storing reusable components; the issues of locating and adapting components are discussed in section 3.3.

We end this subsection with the following guidelines.

CC1: *Provide domain analysis results within the reuse framework—explicitly and/or implicitly.*

CC2: *Make careful assessments, including financial predictions, in deciding whether to develop a reusable component.*

CC3: *Prepare for reuse all more-abstract life-cycle representations of a reusable component (e.g., prepare requirements specification for a high-level design).*

CC4: *Record and supply adaptation suggestions with a reusable component.*

CC5: *Generalize a reusable component to the extent practical during its preparation.*

CC6: *State as a requirement the reuse of software and/or the creation of reusable software.*

3.2.2 Requirements and Designs
3.2.2.1 Overview

Relative to products for reuse, Tracz (1990) gives two "rules of thumb": (1) separate context from content and concept and (2) factor out commonality (i.e., isolate change). Some context information must be supplied at implementation time (e.g., operating system or hardware dependencies). Content pertains to the algorithm and dataflow aspects, and the concept is represented by the functional specification. These suggested "rules" could be beneficial in any software engineering project, but especially so when reuse is anticipated. The approach of separating context (i.e., application environment and machine environment) from the functionality of reusable software, should improve the likelihood of reuse without modification. The aspect of factoring out commonality can lead directly to reuse, and can preclude use and maintenance of redundant code.

In order to reuse designs, they must be machine manipulable. Tracz cites two examples of software reuse based on designs: the DESIRE system at MCC, and the 50 Steps per Module system at Toshiba (where an expert system is used to generate C, Fortran, or Ada code from low-level design data-flow charts, and where reverse engineering is used to prepare data-flow diagrams from existing software).

Tracz states that reuse of specifications is possible within narrow application domains. He cites success at IBM in Owego in reusing avionics specifications (specifically, DOD-STD-2167 System Requirements Specifications). These specifications are prepared as highly parameterized documents with empty tables and missing parameter values. A systems analyst reuses these specifications by use of an application generator, which takes the analyst's input values for tables and parameters, reads the documents, and builds the data structures necessary to drive the supporting software.

Tracz seems less optimistic about the reuse of software for different problem definitions—although parameterization can allow a single module to be generalized over a set of solutions, provided that context is separated from content. He also encourages the use of hypertext to depict relationships (traceability) of different artifacts.

Reuse of domain knowledge is a very high level of reuse and can give extremely important leverage in productivity and quality. As we noted in section 3.1, a domain language is a very high level language incorporating knowledge of the objects, operations, and relationships within a domain; such a language can serve as a specification language for use in constructing systems in the domain (Prieto-Diaz 1987). This is reuse of "meta-requirements," in a sense. The software architectures for a given domain, as discussed in section 3.1, also embody much in the way of requirements and design, and use of the architecture results in reuse of requirements and design. Domain analysis information is an important ingredient in the decision process concerning preparation of reusable components. That is, the required functionality within a domain, as reflected by the domain analysis, helps determine whether a candidate component's functionality is likely to be needed for reuse.

Horowitz and Munson (1984) discuss reusable designs, stating that the essential idea is to study a particular application domain in a formal way (i.e., perform a domain analysis), leading to an understanding of the domain and to various outputs that describe concepts and processes of the domain. (See section 3.1.) The next step is to use the artifacts as the basis for automating the generation of software for the domain. Horowitz and Munson cite compiler generation as a domain for which reusable designs have successfully resulted in widely used parser generators and compiler-compilers (which, though feasible, have met with less success in practice). Backus-Naur Form (BNF) is a "specification language" for this domain; it is used to formally characterize a language's syntax. Another widely known example of design reuse is that of discrete-event simulation, for which many very high level languages have been created, embodying concepts that are common to most or all simulations (e.g., simulated-time management, limited-resource management, etc.). Horowitz and Munson also mention parameterized systems as a candidate all-encompassing approach for a domain. While not detracting from the significance of parameterized systems in smaller contexts, they conclude that this approach is too unwieldy for broadly-based applications development; they discuss an example to support their conclusion.

Horowitz and Munson discuss the work of Neighbors relative to the Draco system (e.g., see Neighbors 1984). This system is intended to aid the translation of a domain specification into an executable program. Horowitz and Munson summarize the steps required in building a software system by use of Draco, as follows:

1. Determine the domain for analysis.
2. Do a domain analysis.
3. Create a domain language and library of concepts.
4. Create a parser and prettyprinter for concepts expressed in the domain language.
5. Define transformations that work from constructs of the output language.
6. Design a specific computerized system using the domain language. Then pass it to Draco, which will translate it into an executable form.

They summarize a similar approach taken by Rice (1981); he advocates the creation and use of an automatic software generation system (ASGS). Such a system would consist of a requirements statement language, an analyzer for the language, and translations of the language program statements to executable code (Rice used Fortran as the target language). Horowitz and Munson observe that the approaches of both Rice and Neighbors critically depend upon the quality of the domain analysis, the ease of use and appropriateness of the resulting language, and the quality of the support system and the resulting executable code. Both Neighbors and Rice report examples of successful use of their methodologies.

Application generators have been available commercially for many years, primarily in the areas of report generation and/or small-scale database manipulation; Horowitz and Munson (1984) provide a partial list of available products and summarize typical steps in the use of such generators. They note that the two basic elements of such systems are (a) a nonprocedural language designed for use by a nontechnical person and (b) built-in knowledge about an existing database management system or about the specification of files on the computer it is running on. These systems typically generate COBOL code; they relieve the user of debugging at the programming language level, generating correct code in a shorter period than could be achieved by conventional programming.

Wegner (1984) observes that application generators strive for reusability in a domain that is narrower than a general-purpose programming language but broader than a specific application. Application generators effect reuse of a mechanism for generating software components and an environment to support generated components. Wegner correctly notes that a deep understanding of a problem domain is necessary to effectively choose a domain for the generator and to design the generic program generator and a prompt-based parameter interface.

So-called fourth-generation languages are of many kinds and include application generators as one category. Martin (1985) discusses fourth-generation languages (4GLs), offering the following properties which should be satisfied by any language to be called a 4GL:

1. It is user-friendly.
2. A nonprofessional programmer can obtain results with it.
3. It employs a database management system directly.
4. Programs for most applications can be created with one order of magnitude fewer instructions than with COBOL.
5. Nonprocedural code is used, where possible.
6. It makes intelligent default assumptions about what the user wants, where possible.
7. It is designed for on-line operation.
8. It enforces or encourages structured code.

9. It makes it easy to understand and maintain another person's code.
10. Non-data processing users can learn a subset of the language in a two-day training course.
11. It is designed for easy debugging.
12. Prototypes can be created and modified quickly.
13. Results can be obtained in one order of magnitude less time than with COBOL or PL/I for most applications.

Martin mentions that 4GLs cannot create all types of applications—i.e., they are not general purpose. While, as he says, some may object to this, it is through such application-specific software reuse that we can achieve the greater productivity desired. Martin lists the following categories for 4GLs: simple-query languages, complex-query-and-update languages, report generators, graphics languages, decison-support languages, application generators, specification languages, very high level programming languages, parameterized application packages, and application languages.

Lubars and Harandi (1989) describe the knowledge-based environment, IDeA (Intelligent Design Aid), that supports reuse of software designs. Design components are abstracted into the form of design schemas; other reusable information includes rules for design specialization and refinement, domain-oriented data object descriptions, domain attributes for data objects and design schemas, and pointers to reusable templates and code. These components are organized into abstraction hierarchies.

Data-flow descriptions are used to help identify candidate design schemas; the approach used is to seek design schemas that satisfy the requirements of the input and output data objects. The underlying assumption is that it is often easier to describe a function's data objects than to describe the function itself. User-imposed constraints are included with schema constraints, and determination is made whether a candidate design satisfies constraints.

IDeA supports a refinement paradigm of software development in which specification and design occur in parallel. The design process can thus be used as a means to check completeness and consistency of specifications. By addressing reuse early in the development process, leverage may be gained from reuse of available components for later phases; for example, design schemas may point to reusable code, software templates, or program designs that can be used to create executable code and/or prototypes.

The next section addresses the important topic of object-oriented approaches to life-cycle activities—especially requirements and designs. In section 3.2.6 we discuss the approach taken to design reuse at Ericsson Telecom.

We end this section by suggesting the following guidelines.

CC7: *In preparing components for reuse, seek to separate functionality from context, and to factor out commonality.*

CC8: *Seek to ease the adaptation effort for specifications and designs by utilizing as much as possible such technologies as application generators, transformation systems, parameterization, and knowledge-based approaches.*

3.2.2.2 Object-Oriented Approaches

Object-oriented design (OOD) is an increasingly important process and promises increased software reuse. Booch (1987a) combines OOD with component reuse through use of the Ada programming language and has spurred a great deal of interest in reuse. McKay (1989) has proposed an object-oriented approach to software development and maintenance, with an automated, knowledge-based approach to identification of reuse opportunities.

Lieberherr and Riel (1988) have designed the Demeter system based on OOD, coupled with parameterized classes. They seek to "grow" software, as recommended by Brooks (1987) through inheritance and parameterization, rather than to build or to create software.

Kaiser and Garlan (1987) have sought to improve OOD for reuse by devising a notation (called MELD) that is independent of any object-oriented language (and would be translated into a conventional programming language). Their system supports composition of components through merging of data structures and methods from two or more "features" (their name for reusable building blocks similar in concept to Ada packages). They employ inheritance and data structure/behavior encapsulation from OOD.

Rogerson and Bailin (1987) conducted an experiment in reuse based on OOD versus functional decomposition and determined that it is easier to detect reusability within a given context for objects (which they represented as Ada packages). Bailin (Bailin 1987; Bailin and Moore 1987) describes an object-oriented approach to software development incorporating reuse that was devised by Computer Technology Associates, Inc. for GSFC. They anticipated that OOD could foster reuse and recommended that GSFC pursue the approach. They have developed the Software Reuse Environment (SRE), consisting of an OOD facility, a reuse database, and search and navigate functions. The OOD facility is the user front-end; it provides graphics support for diagram representation, automatically creates a first approximation to an OOD for annotated data-flow diagrams, and assesses the quality of hierarchies of object diagrams (by means of the design quality assessor). The reuse database is structured by means of semantic networks that relate objects by keywords and associations, constituting a "faceted classification scheme" (Prieto-Diaz and Freeman 1987). Navigation functions permit a user to begin with a specified product or keyword and to move through the reuse database examining relationships and attributes of reusable objects for possible reuse.

Bailin (1989) is also performing research toward applying an object-oriented approach to requirements specification with the intention that the object-oriented specification lead smoothly to OOD and thus to programming in Ada or some other high-level language. He suggests using this method rather than structured analysis when the use of OOD is anticipated. Domain analysis may be viewed as a life-cycle phase occurring prior to requirements determination (Kang 1989; Prieto-Diaz 1987). Domain analysis is discussed in section 3.1. Domain analysis would not precede each requirements determination activity, but rather its output (i.e., domain model and domain architecture) would serve as input to the requirements determination activity for numerous software development projects.

Deutsch (1989) provides a discussion of Smalltalk-80 relative to software reuse. He states, "We believe that interface design and functional factoring constitute the key intellectual content of software and that they are far more difficult to create or recreate than code. For these reasons, we see the reuse of interfaces and factoring as the critical problem in software reuse." His emphasis on interface rather than code stems from his observation that reusing an interface allows the client code, the implementation code, or both to change, while reusing code means that the code stays the same and only the client changes. He characterizes conventional (non-object-oriented) languages as having a strong linkage between the client/service relationship, encapsulation, and the caller/callee relationship, noting that the following are essentially equivalent: (a) X is a client of Y; (b) X has no access to the implementation of Y; (c) X calls routines in Y. He notes that this is true of Ada, as well as for most previous languages—even though in Ada a reused interface may contain types, parametric values, and procedures. The object-oriented approach expands on the caller/callee relationship by supporting dynamic actions of the following kinds:

- A client may instantiate an existing class to produce a new object and interact with the object by sending messages to it. This is similar to (but more general than) library reuse with conventional languages.

- A client may supply an instance X of one of its own classes as a parameter to an existing object Y, expecting that Y will send agreed-upon messages to X. Y is referred to as the framework, and the client is called an internal client. This is a generalization of procedure parameters in conventional languages, and it achieves call-by-name parameter passing.
- A client may define a subclass of an existing class, supplying additional or specialized functionality (referred to as inheritance). Again, the existing class is called the framework, and the client an internal client. There is no feature of conventional languages that fully corresponds to this; record variants provide a limited form of the capability.

These mechanisms promote reuse by means of interface abstraction—use of the interface does not require knowledge of the implementation. Smalltalk-80 is one language embodying these mechanisms, although the standard definition of the language does not support multiple inheritance. While Ada and Modula-2 (for example) support a degree of interface abstraction, more concreteness is necessary in that to invoke an operation on an object it is necessary to state the name of the operation (i.e., procedure), taking data types into account when the (invoking) code is written. Deutsch observes that a reused (object-oriented) framework has three different interfaces: (a) the interface that the reused framework supplies to its external clients (i.e., to its instantiators), which is the same for all reuses; (b) the interface between the framework and its internal clients (i.e., its subclasses or parametrizers), which is also defined by the framework and stays the same for all reuses; and (c) the interface each external client has with the combination of the framework and internal clients. The latter will vary if external messages are implemented by the internal client. Such messages will be different for each internal client. Deutsch's intent is to promote reuse of designs by means of frameworks of partially completed code. His idea is that a framework binds certain choices about state partitioning and control flow and that the (re)user completes or extends the framework to produce an actual application. It could be that a single class is partially abstract, and a user would determine subclasses or parameters to complete the implementation. More complicated systems may require hierarchies of framework classes, which are completed for actual applications. Deutsch gives several examples of the use of Smalltalk-80 in achieving reuse.

Jette and Smith (1989) discuss the benefit of object-oriented programming for reuse, based on their work at Schlumberger in developing oil well analysis tools. Their system, HyperClass, is a user interface tool kit that encapsulates knowledge about user interfaces in terms of editors and editor parts; they reuse HyperClass's encapsulated knowledge for extending the kernel (to provide additional interface mechanisms) and for implementing application-specific extensions.

These writers view objects as being (or being treated as) atomic components of systems—the objects represent real-world atomic entities. The intent is that the objects may be composed with little or no alteration to represent a new or altered system. They view object-oriented programming as encouraging a declarative style of programming, in which much of the state or control information is stored and recorded as a part of a class or instance definition. This supports specialization at runtime by means of the data bindings found in instance or class variables. They emphasize that object-oriented programming reuses abstractions, not just the code or the leaf nodes in a hierarchy. And, even if a particular leaf node cannot be reused, one may be able to back off to an abstraction and reuse it. Their experience indicates that as an object-oriented system matures, less and less code is required to add new extensions.

Jette and Smith (1989) mention that an advantage to designing systems with reuse in mind is that the systems will have a common look and feel with respect to internal interfaces as well as the user interface, since so many components and protocols are common. This should make maintenance simpler due to commonality of components. However, extensive use of inheritance and message passing will increase the need for good browsing tools to isolate which class/method is responsible for a problem. They mention that to maximize reuse one must often go back and rethink the design and the code to be reused—it is experience that makes this work. They also believe that additional future work on tools to support the development/reuse process can help tremendously; they mention as an example a tool that makes explicit the protocols used and the need for a powerful browser with inferencing capabilities. They also mention the tradeoff required between a highly modular design that maximizes reuse and one that maximizes runtime performance; the costs of modularity include message passing to invoke fine-grained methods and class instantiation. They expect better object-oriented compilation techniques to help. This disadvantage is offset by the benefit of very short development times for customized application interfaces (a few days or weeks).

Biggerstaff and Perlis (1989b) make several observations about the work reported by Jette and Smith (1989). They say that HyperClass has been used to solve real-world problems longer than perhaps any other object-oriented system except Smalltalk. The difficult requirement of integrating non-object-oriented tools was successfully accomplished. They had to extend the object-oriented model to accommodate "persistent objects" (objects that span multiple application program executions), thus combining database and object technologies. They have also successfully focused on application domain reuse. Biggerstaff and Perlis consider the experience with HyperClass to be valuable as a baseline for others considering such activities.

Meyer (1987) stresses the importance of extendibility as a companion requirement to reusability, defining extendibility as the ease with which software can be modified to reflect changes in specification. His main thesis is "that object-oriented design is the most promising technique now known for attaining the goals of extendibility and reusability." He makes the point that programmers tend to do the same kinds of things time and time again, but they are not exactly the same things. In practice so many details may change as to render useless any simple-minded attempt at capturing commonality. He cites as an example that all sequential tables have similarities, but observes that if we really want to write carefully organized libraries of reusable software elements, we must be able to use commonalities at all levels of abstraction. He emphasizes that such issues are purely technical—no management approaches, per se, can help.

Meyer (1987) states that for a subprogram library to be effective for reuse where a set of individual problems can be identified, the following limitations must hold:

- Every instance of each problem should be identifiable with a small set of parameters.
- The individual problems should be clearly distinct. Any significant commonality that might exist cannot be put to good use, except by reusing some of the design.
- No complex data structures should be involved, because they would have to be distributed among the routines and the conceptual autonomy of modules would be lost.

He illustrates the problem by mentioning the table-searching example again, stating that we can either write a single subprogram or set of subprograms, each corresponding to a special case. The approach of a single subprogram will be essentially a very large case statement, very complex and difficult to use, and very cumbersome to modify. The approach of a set of subprograms will mean having many that are similar looking—such as search subprograms for sequential arrays and sequential linked lists. Yet even though there are similarities, there is no simple way to make use of the similarities.

Meyer says that languages like Ada and Modula-2 offer a first step toward a solution since they offer a structuring mechanism at a higher level than a subprogram (i.e., the package for Ada and the module for Modula-2). Thus the package/module can be devoted to an entire data structure and its associated operations, e.g., a data structure for a table and the routines that create and delete tables and insert and delete elements in a table. Thus we can "keep under one roof a set of related routines that pertain to a specific implementation of a data abstraction" (Meyer 1987). Meyer characterizes this mechanism as useful but limited. Useful because encapsulating related features helps implementors and users; limited because the mechanism does not offer any help in capturing common features and thus does not reduce the amount of software that must be developed.

Overloading and genericity are additional features that promote reusability. Overloading permits more than one meaning to be given to a name. Ada and Algol 68 offer this capability. For example, search subprograms for various data structures could all be called "Search," and an invocation like SEARCH(x,t) would cause the correct routine to be chosen based on the types of x and t (Meyer 1987). Genericity allows modules to have generic parameters that represent types; Ada and Clu offer this feature. By use of generic parameters, one module may suffice instead of a group of modules differing only by the type of objects manipulated. Both overloading and genericity offer help for reuse (Meyer 1987):

- With overloading, the client programmer may write the same code when using different implementations of the same data abstraction, as provided by different modules.
- With genericity, the implementor may write a single module for all instances of the same implementation of a data abstraction applied to various types of objects.

But again, Meyer contends that these techniques do not go far enough toward reusability in that they do not provide enough flexibility (support for a complex hierarchy of representations with different levels of parameterization). Meyer also contends that these techniques force programmers to decide too much too soon (because a given use of either overloading or genericity results in the compiler making one specific instantiated module available for use at runtime). The user doesn't need to know how the resulting module is implemented, but must know, for example, that a search routine is needed for a sequential array rather than a linked-list array. Meyer contends that "true representation independence only happens when a client can write the invocation SEARCH(x,t) and mean, 'look for x in t using the appropriate algorithm for whatever kind of table and element x and t happen to be at the time the invocation is executed.'" He contends that this flexibility is essential for the construction of reusable software elements and that it can only be achieved with OOD.

Meyer (1987) views OOD as a software decomposition technique in which the modular decomposition of a software system is based on the classes of objects the system manipulates, rather than on the functions the system performs (as is true of functional design). His contention is that over time the functions implemented by software are very likely to change, while the objects that are manipulated should remain much the same. For example, Meyer notes that an operating system will always work on devices, memories, processing units, communication channels, etc. Thus it is better for the long term to base decomposition on categories of objects, provided that the object categories are viewed at a sufficiently high level of abstraction.

Meyer discusses the aspect of "sufficiently high level of abstraction" in terms of abstract data types: an abstract data type is a class of objects characterized by the operations available on them and the abstract properties of these operations (Meyer 1987). That is, abstract data types describe classes of objects only through the external properties of the objects and not by means of their internal representation. Meyer considers abstract data types to be useful for software specifications, designs, and implementation, and in particular to be essential to the object-oriented approach. He refines the definition of OOD to "the construction of software systems as structured collections of abstract data type implementations." Meyer makes the point that the object-oriented method identifies modules with implementations of abstract data types; i.e., a single program structure is both a module and type. Such a structure was called a "class" in Simula 67, which was the first object-oriented language. Meyer uses class as the name for this structure in his Eiffel language. In Meyer's view, an Ada package or a Modula-2 module may comprise an implementation of an abstract data type, but cannot be identified with the implementation as is the case with true object-oriented modules. Relative to Meyer's definition of OOD, he emphasizes the words "implementation" and "structured." He emphasizes that a module of an object-oriented program is not an abstract data type, but rather one implementation of an abstract data type; however, the implementation hides implementation details from "clients," permitting only the official specification of the abstract data type to be seen. He emphasizes the word "structured," pointing out that collections of classes may be structured using two different relations: "client" and "inheritance."

The client relation is that of a "user" of an object. In Ada, an object represented as a package could be accessed by a "client" module by stating the package name and the name of a "visible" operation defined within the package. For example, QUEUE.REMOVE(ELT) could invoke the function REMOVE within the package QUEUE, obtaining the element at the "head" of the queue. Meyer's Eiffel language employs similar notation. In Eiffel, a class A may be a user of a class B by having within class A a declaration such as bb: B. An example given by Meyer (1987) is a class BINARY_SEARCH_TREE, permitting operations such as create and insert. A client class X would contain a declaration such as bb: BINARY_SEARCH_TREE. The statement bb.create within class X would cause table bb to actually be allocated; the statement bb.insert(elt) would cause the value of elt to be inserted into bb. The expression bb.size would provide the current size of the table bb. In Eiffel terminology, the permitted operations within a class are called routines and may be either functions (which return a result value) or procedures (which do not return a value). Features of a class are the accessible routines and accessible data structure attributes (e.g., bb.size above). Eiffel accomplishes information hiding within classes by means of the export clause, much the same as Modula-2. The client relation may be depicted diagrammatically by showing a horizontal double arrow from the client class to the servicing class; the classes may be depicted by means of circles or ellipses containing the name of a class.

The inheritance relation is provided in Eiffel, but not in Ada or Modula-2, for example. It is also provided in Simula, in such C-based languages as Objective C and C++, in Object Pascal, Smalltalk, and in Lisp-based languages such as Loops and Flavors (Meyer 1987). For example, the BINARY_SEARCH_TABLE class may be defined as an "heir" to a class TABLE that describes properties of tables independent of representation. The BINARY_SEARCH_TABLE class would inherit all features of TABLE, and add some of its own. In general, a class C defined as an heir of class A has all the features of A, and may add its own features. The "descendants" of a class include its heirs, the heirs of its heirs, etc. Eiffel supports multiple inheritance—i.e., a class C may be heir to classes B and A, thus having all their features, to which it may add its own. The inheritance relation may be depicted diagrammatically by drawing a single, vertical arrow from the heir upward to the inherited class. A brief summary of other characteristics of Eiffel is provided by Meyer (1987).

Meyer considers the combination of OOD and the client and inheritance relations as being key elements in achieving reusability and extendibility. He gives a worked-out example of an interactive full-screen entry system. He begins with a top-down decomposition approach and observes that it is not satisfactory from a reusability standpoint. While his design separated generic aspects from aspects specific to particular applications, a great deal of data sharing occurs throughout all modules. This makes it difficult to implement extensions, requiring modifications throughout the system. Also, subprograms within the structure cannot easily be extracted for use in a reuse library because of their interrelationships with other components.

Meyer (1987) then applies what he calls the law of inversion, "If there is too much data transmission in your routines, then put your routines into your data." That is, follow the object-oriented approach using the most important data structures as the basis for modularization and attach each routine to the data structure to which it applies most closely. Meyer says that for programmers trained in functional approaches "this is as revolutionary as making the Sun orbit Earth!" Meyer goes through a solution to the problem based on OOD, and makes a very good case for the reusability and extendibility of it. Space prohibits further discussion of this problem, but it would be beneficial for interested readers to obtain a copy of this paper and read through his example. It is well written and serves as a good case study of the benefits of OOD.

Meyer (1987) maintains that reusability is essential to better software quality and that the object-oriented approach provides a promising set of solutions. He expresses concern about top-down design being an essential requirement in DOD-STD-2167, "which by the sheer power of its sponsor is bound to have a serious (and, we fear, negative) influence for years to come." He advocates a bottom-up approach to construction of systems by reusing and combining existing software into more and more ambitious systems.

Meyer (1987) believes that overemphasis on management issues is premature. "Its like expecting better hospital management to solve the public hygiene problem 10 years before Pasteur came along! Give your poor, your huddled projects a decent technical environment in the first place. Then worry about whether you are managing them properly."

As Meyer noted, Ada lacks a number of features that are considered desirable for object-oriented implementations. On the other hand, the languages that do provide many object-oriented implementation features do not currently have adequate run-time efficiency for many DOD real-time applications.

There are many implications in the decision to use object oriented approaches. Section 2.2 discussed the software process, and the importance of incorporating reuse. It appears that reuse can be facilitated by object oriented approaches–especially in matching "what you need" to "what you have", relative to reusable components. However, approaches for requirements determination by means of object orientation are immature at this time. Also, existing object-oriented languages are rapidly changing and new languages are appearing.

Organizations with a substantial investment and expertise in functional decomposition methods, should weigh very carefully the decision to go to object-oriented approaches and how best to transition to the new approaches. Also, the nature of object-oriented languages is such that execution-time performance tends to be poorer than for static-binding languages – which could make them unsuitable for some real-time applications. No doubt such concerns will bring about eventual improvements in run-time performance of object-oriented languages.

The current Ada 9X review process is considering possible changes to improve Ada's use in object oriented development. The results of these deliberations will be important to the reuse decision process for some organizations.

Having made these observations, we end this section with the following guideline – which should be understood in view of the observations.

CC9: *Evaluate object-oriented approaches for use in the software process, considering especially the benefits for reusable components.*

3.2.3 Code Components

Reusable code is the most researched of the reuse abstraction levels; more is known about it, more has been written about it, and most software reuse has been based on code. In this section we consider two aspects of reusable code: (1) code component structures and (2) programming style.

3.2.3.1 Code Component Structures

There are two different clearly distinguishable categories of code components for reuse. The first may be called passive components or building blocks, which are used essentially unchanged by means of composition. The second category involves dynamic components or generators, which generate a product for reuse. These components are also spoken of as reusable patterns, and they are very effective when feasible. Biggerstaff and Richter (1987) list generators of two fundamental types: (1) application generators (employing reusable patterns of code) and (2) transformation systems (generating a product by successive application of transformation rules—see Cheatham 1984). Generators by their nature tend to lift the abstraction level for reuse above that of code building blocks. For example, compiler syntax analyzer generators (e.g., YACC) do their work with little need for the user to understand the underlying concepts. Simulation languages/systems constitute another application of reusable patterns to achieve effective leverage (Hooper 1988). Prototyping usually is based on significant reuse of software; it may be based on very high level languages, somewhat like simulation languages, and/or may be based on code blocks. Fourth-generation languages constitute another kind of reusable pattern and also substantially lift the reuse abstraction level. These concepts are discussed further in section 3.2.2.1.

Code blocks for reuse have historically been subprograms (procedures or functions), and now they include Ada packages (collections of reusable subprograms with their encapsulated environment), classes (in the sense of object-oriented programming), and Ada generics. Parameterized code may be based on any of the forms of code blocks just mentioned. Also, code templates may be used, with slots to be filled in by a user to customize for a given application.

Wegner (1984) discusses some important characteristics of components intended for reuse. He describes a component's interface as "what the user sees," noting that syntactic interfaces specify compile-time invariants that determine how components fit together, and that semantic interfaces specify execution-time invariants that determine what the component computes. He suggests viewing the syntactic interface of a subprogram definition as a socket, and thus viewing subprogram calls as plugs that are "plugged in" at the time of a call. In this vein, the actual parameters may be viewed as prongs of a plug whose size and shape depend on the parameter type; of course, the number and type of these prongs must correspond to the slots in the interface socket. While we find it desirable to precisely specify the "sockets and plugs" (i.e., strong typing), as in Ada, it is limiting from the standpoint of reuse. Wegner states that, in principle, a good compiler should be able to transform strongly typed modules into efficient untyped internal modules, but we do not yet know how to do this well.

Another important characteristic of reusable components is abstraction. Wegner (1984) quotes Hoare as follows:

> In the development of the understanding of complex phenomena, the most powerful tool available to the human intellect is abstraction. Abstraction arises from a recognition of similarities between certain objects, situations, or processes in the

real world and the decision to concentrate on these similarities
and to ignore, for the time being, their differences.

The idea of function abstraction is that a function f may be specified entirely by input-output relationships: every input x determines
a unique output $f(x)$ that depends on x alone. The user of a component based on function abstraction need not know how the function
is implemented. The implementation is hidden, and the user is aware
only of the input/output relationships designated by the interface
specification.

Another approach to abstraction discussed by Wegner is referred
to as data abstraction, in which data as well as function implementations may be hidden from the user. With this approach $f(x)$ may
depend on a "remembered" internal state as well as on the input parameter x. The hidden data characterizes the current state, which
may be transformed by means of the set of internal (hidden) operations. Components that incorporate this approach are usually referred
to as "objects" and are said to be object oriented.

A third abstraction approach discussed by Wegner is process abstraction, which is like data abstraction with the additional feature
of permitting an independently executing thread of control. Process
abstractions make use of ports through which users obtain synchro-
nized access to resources of the process; access requests are placed
in a queue until the process is ready to handle them. The two categories of processes are concurrent processes (which may communicate
through shared global data) and distributed processes (which communicate only by message passing). It is evident that processes are
also object-oriented. Wegner summarizes the three abstraction mechanisms as follows: functions are abstract operations; data abstractions
are abstract variables; and processes are abstract computers.

As can be inferred from the above discussion, an "object" is a
software component having a hidden state and a set of operations
or capabilities for transforming the state (Wegner 1984). The term
object is used relative to programming languages, databases, and operating systems. Smalltalk is perhaps the best-known object-oriented
language. Numerous others, such as C++, Objective C, and Eiffel (Meyer 1987), are appearing. Booch (1987a, 1987b) promotes
the use of Ada for object-oriented development of reusable components. Classic–Ada, available from Software Productivity Solutions,
Inc. (SPS), adds inheritance and dynamic binding to Ada.

The recent past has produced better programming languages for
reusability support—especially Ada. Modula-2, Borland's Pascal 5.5,
and various other available languages also have some good features.
But the DOD mandate for use of Ada doubtless makes Ada the lan-

guage of choice for many large software projects. Ada has very strong features for reuse, such as the package (information hiding, encapsulation, etc.) and generics.

3.2.3.2 Programming Style

Soloway and Ehrlich (1984) conducted studies to determine how program comprehension is impacted by programming style. They believe that expert programmers are distinguished from novice programmers in that experts have at least two types of knowledge that novices do not have:

- Programming plans: program fragments that represent stereotypical action sequences in programming;
- Rules of programming discourse: rules that specify programming conventions (e.g., a variable should be given a meaningful name relative to its function) and bring about expectations by the programmer about programs.

The study was designed to evaluate the claim that expert programmers possess programming plans and discourse rules, and if programs violate such plans or rules they should be harder for an expert programmer to understand than if they did conform to the plans/rules. "Planlike" and "unplanlike" versions of programs were presented to both novice and expert programmers, and the programmers were asked to perform such actions as recalling a small program verbatim or filling in a blank line with code that best completes a program. The finding was that when programs were planlike, an expert performed significantly better than a novice in completing a program, but given an unplanlike program, experts performed at essentially the same level as novices. Further findings indicated that an expert programmer could recall an entire program with significantly fewer "readings" when it was planlike than when it was not. Soloway and Ehrlich mention that such measures as number of lines of code or Halstead metrics would not predict the differences in performance they obtained, and they conclude that their study supports the claim that knowledge of programming conventions can have a significant impact on program comprehension.

The practical significance of this work to software reuse is that programmers consistently "reuse" skeletal program sequences to accomplish needed functionality and read programs assuming that certain conventions have been used. Thus programs should be written with conventional style to benefit understandability—and it is especially important to do so if reuse is anticipated.

Biggerstaff and Perlis (1989a) make some insightful observations concerning the need for standards that transcend individual components. This is necessary in order to have the capability to assemble components together based only on their functions, inputs, and outputs. Such a standard for software components is akin to that imposed by hardware component manufacturers so that hardware components can be plugged together. Biggerstaff and Perlis say:

> Herein lies a rule for those who would create libraries of reusable code components. The library should be based on a standard for the domain-specific types of the data consumed and produced by the components in that library. If there is not such an architectural standard that applies across all components in the library, then the level of reuse will be very much less than it could be and very much less than one would like. This observation militates against just finding and throwing together a set of components that have functions more or less covering the needs of the using organization. A library of components that are to be (re)used together needs to be designed according to a common architectural guideline that reflects both the nature of the problem domain (e.g., real-time process control software) as well as the computational needs of the organization.

Basili et al. (1989) have provided a number of guidelines for developing Ada code, based on their research into the impacts for reuse of the strength of data bindings of a module with its environment and on their assessment of effort necessary to transform existing Ada code for reuse in contexts other than the original one. They suggest the following:

- Avoid excessive multiple nesting in any language constructs.
- Avoid using of the USE clause if possible.
- Prevent components from interacting with their outer environment.
- Use appropriate packaging to accommodate reusability.
- Avoid mingling resource units with application-specific context.
- Avoid literal values.
- Keep interfaces abstract.

Guidelines that are Ada-specific are presented in Appendix B, Guidelines for Reusable Ada code.

Berard (EVB 1987) stresses the importance of good coding style for reuse—e.g., using meaningful identifiers; avoiding literal constants;

using adequate, concise, and precise comments; making frequent and appropriate use of packages; isolating and clearly identifying environmentally dependent code; and, modules should be highly cohesive and loosely coupled. In general, the approaches that promote understanding for maintainability serve equally well for reuse.

Barsotti and Wilkinson (1987) argue that reuse of code is essentially a byproduct of quality and maintainability. To this end they recommend

- using certified algorithms
- defining error handling
- defining exceptional conditions
- establishing explicit interfaces
- developing modular programs
- parameterizing
- providing all test data and reports

They also provide a list of quality criteria: accuracy, application independence, augmentability, completeness, conciseness, consistency, fault tolerance, generality, legibility, self-descriptiveness, simplicity, structuredness, system accessibility, and traceability. They provide precise definitions to all these terms. By application independence they mean nondependency on the database system, microcode, computer architecture, and algorithms (i.e., not independence from an application domain); this thus includes the important criterion of portability. By system accessibility, they mean provision for control and audit of access to the software and data. They indicate that all these criteria support reusability and that all support maintainability except accuracy, application independence, and fault tolerance. Reliability is supported by all except application independence, augmentability, generality, self-descriptiveness, simplicity, and system accessibility. While one could argue with some of these particulars, the concepts are worthwhile. These and other criteria relate to the concept of software metrics—criteria by which the suitability of software may be measured.

St. Dennis (1987) suggests a list of 15 language-independent characteristics of reusable code.

1. Interface is both syntactically and semantically clear.
2. Interface is written at the appropriate (abstract) level.
3. Component does not interfere with its environment.
4. Component is designed as object-oriented; that is, packaged as typed data with procedures and functions that act on the data.

5. Actions based on function results are made at the next higher level.
6. Component incorporates scaffolding for use during building phase.
7. Information needed to use software (specification) should be separate from the details of its implementation (body).
8. Component exhibits high cohesion/low coupling.
9. Component and interface are written to be readable by persons other than the author.
10. Component is written with the right balance between generality and specificity.
11. Component is accompanied by sufficient documentation to make it findable.
12. Component can be used without change or with only minor modifications.
13. Component should be insulated from host/target dependencies and assumptions about its environment; it should be isolated from format and content of information passed through it that it does not use.
14. Component is standardized in the areas of invoking, controlling, and terminating its function; error-handling; and communication and structure.
15. Components should be written to exploit domain of applicability; components should constitute the right abstraction and modularity for the application.

The Ada language is at once a primary motivator of reuse and a primary mechanism for reuse. Ada provides a rich set of features supporting reusability (St. Dennis 1986), including

- packages;
- separate compilation and checking across program units;
- separate specifications and bodies for program units;
- information hiding constructs (e.g., private types);
- generics;
- strong typing.

Ada was designed to promote reliability and maintainability, programming as a human activity, and efficiency. As St. Dennis (1986) notes,

Software reliability, maintainability and efficiency also contribute positively to reuse. Reliability contributes to user confidence in a software component, maintainability to understandability, and efficiency to feasibility for reuse.

As we have noted, a number of reuse guidebooks are available (e.g., Wald 1986; ISEC 1985; Braun, Goodenough, and Eaves 1985; St. Dennis 1986). Of these, St. Dennis provides by far the most extensive set of guidelines for writing reusable Ada source code. Most of the guidelines in Appendix B are from St. Dennis—and, we have included most of St. Dennis' guidelines. The "Exceptions" guidelines, and a few others, are from ISEC. Most of the guidelines suggested by Basili et al. (1989) are included in the list.

The guidelines provided in Appendix B are grouped by Ada features and issues. St. Dennis relates these guidelines to his reusability characteristics. He presents detailed discussions and examples for the guidelines obtained from that document. The reader is encouraged to consult St. Dennis (1986) and ISEC (1985) for further information.

Another reference for Ada-based software reuse is Gautier and Wallis (1990). This book consists of a collection of papers produced by the Ada-Europe Working Group on Software Reuse. A wide range of topics is discussed in these papers including reuse strategies using Ada, component engineering with Ada, and organizing component libraries. There is also a summary of some reuse experiences with Ada. Reuse guidelines are included under the headings of design, generic components, exceptions, and tasks.

The following guidelines briefly summarize our observations.

CC10: *Supply reusable code in the form of a generator or a transformation system for greater reuse leverage, when practical.*

CC11: *In preparing code blocks, use generics, parameterized procedures, and code templates for greater reuse generality, as appropriate.*

CC12: *Emphasize good programming style in developing reusable code, creating code exhibiting understandability, reliability, and maintainability.*

CC13: *Emphasize Ada and other programming languages that are suitable for reusable code.*

CC14: *Establish a set of organizational guidelines for code development.*

3.2.4 Component Quality

If software reuse is to be successful, the available reusable components must be worthy of user confidence. Fairley et al. (1989)

examined six successful software reuse projects and observed several factors the projects had in common. One of the factors was that each component had to meet a set of standards to ensure the highest possible quality before the component was placed in a repository or reused. Numerous aspects bear upon the achievement and maintenance of component quality, including the understandability and completeness of requirements and designs, the quality of documentation, programming style, and ultimately the correct performance of the reused software. Two underlying issues that require special attention are component verification and validation (V&V) and configuration management.

The importance of the configuration management issue is well known to software engineers. Mechanisms for configuration management are practiced effectively by many organizations. Since having the trust and confidence of reusers is critical, great emphasis should be placed on workable configuration management procedures.

As we noted in chapter 2, there is typically some resistance to using software created outside an organization. Every effort must be made to overcome any legitimate concerns about the quality and reliability of such software. Another facet of this issue is the potential liability the creating organization may have. In most respects this is an unresolved legal issue (chapter 2); but at a minimum the creating organization's reputation and business potential are affected by the perception of users of its products.

The issue of component V&V is especially significant for reusable software. Bullard et al. (1989) have studied this issue under the AIRMICS Ada Reuse and Metrics project. As they observe, in the past the focus of V&V was to determine whether software met its specification within a specific environment. In the case of reusable software, however, the software may be reused in numerous different environments. They differentiate between (1) the "machine environment" (physical hardware and virtual machine incorporating operating system and any run time environment and conventions set up by the compiler) and (2) the "application environment" (application-programmer-written components with which the reusable software component is to be used). They note that "porting" a component is changing its machine environment and "adapting" a component is changing its application environment. This gives rise to "portability errors" and "adaptability errors," both of which must be avoided with reusable software. Portability and adaptability effectively define two different interfaces: a "machine interface" and an "application interface." Reuse errors may be usefully considered relative to these interfaces.

Bullard et al. (1989) state that portability errors are contained entirely within the reusable component and can be detected during unit testing (as opposed to integration testing). Adaptability errors, on the other hand, span the application interface and represent only potential errors in the component, since it is impossible to anticipate all potential application environments—i.e., application interfaces. Adaptability problems thus must be considered at systems integration time although the potential for an adaptability error may be detectable by considering the component alone. The Ada language definition considers components with portability errors to be erroneous (Bullard et al.). Many such errors can be detected statically, since language constructs that permit some compiler or operating system latitude are known. On the other hand, adaptability errors are not amenable to formal verification techniques, since any error is relative to a specific application environment. Whereas portability has been extensively studied and is relatively well understood (including problems with specific programming languages), adaptability errors are much more difficult to resolve.

Bullard et al. (1989) give a good discussion of approaches for detecting reuse errors; in brief, they include (1) testing a reusable module in a variety of actual environments (which cannot be all-encompassing), (2) testing the module with simulated application environments, (3) considering static measures of portability and adaptability, (4) conducting mutation analysis, and (5) conducting constraint-based analysis.

Bullard et al. (1989) suggest three general categories for portability errors; they also suggest using these categories to recognize or to detect portability errors and to remove or adequately document them.

CLASSIFICATION OF PORTABILITY ERRORS

    (a) Types of Application
        (i) numerical (e.g., errors related to convergence, error propagation, floating point precision, overflow treatment, or byte alignment)
        (ii) multitasking (e.g., errors related to incompatibility of code from different compilers, timing and synchronizing problems, shared variable use, or use of machine priorities)
        (iii) dynamic memory allocation (e.g., problems due to space overflow, machine differences in available memory, or method of allocating pointers)

(iv) systems programming (e.g., absolute location specification, object representation, maximum object space allocation, or unchecked conversions)

(b) Manner of Error Detection
   (i) static analysis (e.g., unchecked deallocation, machine code insertions, use of machine constants, or dependency on order of evaluation or on a particular memory initialization policy)
   (ii) simulation (e.g., method of interacting with the environment at execution time—allocating and laying out storage, passing parameters, elaborating library units, or synchronization of multiple processors)
   (iii) mutation analysis (e.g., problems detectable through manipulation of input, whether an exception is raised on overflow, or whether a machine rounds or truncates unrepresentable values)
   (iv) constraint analysis (e.g., the need for at least a certain precision for floating point calculations or the need for a very large amount of memory for dynamic allocation)

(c) Language Constructs
   Bullard et al. (1989) cite references to the literature concerning portability problems associated with specific Ada constructs.

The following categorization of adaptability errors is also from Bullard et al. (1989).

CLASSIFICATION OF ADAPTABILITY ERRORS

(a) Architectural Concerns (Booch 1987a)
   (i) concurrency (sequential, guarded, concurrent, or multiple)
   (ii) space utilization (unbounded or bounded)
   (iii) space reclamation (unmanaged, managed, or controlled)
   (iv) iterator availability (whether an operation is available to yield the elements of an object of an abstract data type)

(b) Implementation Concerns
   (i) order of evaluation errors
   (ii) aliasing errors
   (iii) domain errors (e.g., a subprogram defined on only values within a certain range)
   (iv) protocol errors (e.g., a component with a retained state, subject to constraints—such as no more POPs than PUSHes for a stack component)

Bullard et al. note that, in the case of implementation concerns (item b), the common concern is that the component is inadvertently designed to allow a client application to misuse the component; i.e., potential error exists. They note that the realization of the error exists somewhere across the application interface in the application environment itself, otherwise the error is either a portability error (as in the case of aliasing, order of evaluation, etc.) or a traditional error (as in the case of a domain error). Thus traditional V&V techniques are of little use in detecting the problems.

The work reported here from Bullard et al. (1989) points up the difficulty in determining reuse errors—especially adaptability errors; certifying a component as error free relative to any arbitrary environment is impossible for the general case. Thus the goal should be to develop components with portability and adaptability considerations built in—by means of explicit specification of portability and adaptability requirements, isolating portability-related code, and building defensive assertions into the code relative to adaptability.

Another important aspect of software quality assessment is the recorded experiences of users of library components. We consider this in section 3.3. Quality assurance activities are considered essential in organizations practicing software engineering. Because of the critical importance of the correctness of reusable software, even greater emphasis should be placed on the scrutiny of reusable components by a quality assurance group. ISEC (1985) suggests the use of a "reusability checklist" by the quality assurance group.

We conclude this section with the following guidelines, prefaced either with "Q" (for quality) or "V" (for V&V). The V&V guidelines were adapted from Bullard et al. (1989).

Q1: *Set standards to be met by all library components.*

Q2: *Emphasize stringent V&V for reusable components, stressing portability and adaptability.*

Q3: *Emphasize enforcement of standards and practices by the quality assurance group; employ a reusability checklist.*

Q4: *Establish and operate an effective configuration management program for the reuse library.*

V1: *State environment compatibility explicitly in the requirements specification.*

V2: *Specify constraints on the use of reusable components as assertions; include assertions within the component specification and (if practical) within the executable code.*

V3: *Construct code for portability and adaptability (rather than attempting to isolate inadequacies by testing).*

V4: *Parameterize specifications that are dependent on the machine environment so that the behavior of the component is expressed relative to a part of the machine environment.*

V5: *Classify reusable components along each of the dimensions of concurrency, space utilization, space reclamation, and iterator availability; make the classification a part of the component specification.*

V6: *Use suggested classification of reuse errors to recognize or to detect errors automatically; remove errors if possible, or adequately document their existence for location and modification when necessary.*

V7: *Employ a comprehensive testing method, consisting of a combination of approaches, to detect reuse errors (including simulation of the execution environment, static analysis, mutation analysis, and constraint-based analysis).*

V8: *Include adequacy criteria that reduce the amount of testing needed and provide a measure of a test suite's effectiveness.*

3.2.5 Classifying and Storing Components

Having determined that components will be made available for reuse, it is necessary to classify each component according to some taxonomy and to store the component in an on-line library for reuse. An organization must make decisions early-on about the scheme(s) for classification, and carefully classify each component for reuse. The decision has many ramifications, since the approach for locating and retrieving available components (section 3.3) is largely determined by the approach for classifying and storing.

Considerable research and experimentation have been conducted in this aspect of reuse repository operation. Prieto-Diaz and Freeman (1987) have developed the faceted classification method, based on ideas from library science. Each component is characterized by a sextuple consisting of

<function,objects,medium,system type,functional area,setting>.

They incorporate the idea of conceptual closeness to give a user a measure of how closely an available component corresponds to a specified facet during retrieval.

Ramamoorthy, Garg and Prakash (1986) have selected the entity-relationship-attribute (ERA) model as the basis for cataloging and retrieving reusable components. They use such attributes as classification (requirements, design, source, test case, document, library, and object code); hierarchy (family, member, layer, module, and procedure); and nonfunctional attributes such as reliability, memory requirements, performance, and metrics concerning quality and complexity. Their relations include classification-to-classification, hierarchical_level-to-hierarchical_level, use of resources, etc. They have developed the Entity Specification Language (ESL) to support software personnel in inserting, modifying, or deleting information in the library.

Mittermeir and Rossak (1987) have proposed library organizations that they call software archives (to support the retrieval of design units for potential reuse) and software bases (to support retrieval of executable code). They represent the structure of a software archive by a four-dimensional "cube," the dimensions being decomposition, representational form, association (application-dependent links), and generalization/specialization. This structure thus uses links among components to represent knowledge about interrelationships.

Wood and Sommerville (1988) have taken a cataloging approach based on natural language processing—specifically the idea of concept case frames. They rely on a system that creates component-descriptor frames (their version of concept-case frames) by means of a form-filling interface. There is a component-descriptor frame for each basic function that software performs—representing a class of conceptually similar verbs (e.g., search, look, and find). There are four slots in each frame corresponding to a library component, objects manipulated by the component, objects produced as a result of the action, and objects that provide a context for the action. An example is (in order) a report generator, a personnel record, a formatted report, and directives that describe the desired report. This organization was devised to improve the process of retrieval (section 3.3.2).

The RAPID Center Project (discussed in section 1.4) being pursued by SofTech under contract to the U.S. Army ISEC, is developing the RAPID Center Library (RCL) System (Guerrieri 1988). Classification is based on the faceted classification scheme of Prieto-Diaz and Freeman (1987). User activities supported relative to reusable software components are identification, extraction, and report generation. The RAPID Center will also provide guidance to users by technical staff.

Gagliano, Fraser, and Owen (1989) have developed an experimental reuse library system, based in part on Prieto-Diaz's work, for reusable Ada components. They are developing several tools to ease the development and use of a reuse library.

For effective retrieval, the library should somehow represent relationship information between components (e.g., between a design component and the corresponding code, between a system specification and a subsystem specification, between two components that are related by reuse potential within a given application domain, and between two components such that one is a specialization of the other). Research has been conducted to examine appropriate structures for database support for software reuse—i.e., to determine how best to use the knowledge and systems of database management and information retrieval to support the creation and use of software repositories. Bein, Drew, and King (1989) suggest the use of both the object-oriented data model and the semantic data model in creating and managing libraries for software reuse. They cite the need for composite objects, multiple inheritance, representation of relationships (one-to-one, one-to-many, and many-to-many), and monitoring of data integrity. Relative to database functionality, they cite the need for dynamic schema evolution, transparent operation within distributed environments, version control, security and authorization support, and transaction management and concurrency control.

Frakes and Nejmeh (1987) take an entirely different approach to the structure of reuse libraries, arguing that with the advent of fast special-purpose hardware for information retrieval (IR), it is feasible to use IR approaches for textual-based component search and retrieval, rather than use elaborate database organizations. We will consider these ideas further in section 3.3.2.

Regarding the question of what documentation should be provided on-line with each reusable component, Van Scoy and Plinta (1989) suggest two levels of information for code components:

1. high-level description of the functionality provided by the component;
2. detailed description of the components.

The high-level description is assumed to describe the component's functionality in terms familiar to prospective users. The approach of domain-specific libraries lends itself to this end. The detailed description should include the following seven items. Items 1 through 6 are from Van Scoy and Plinta (1989) and item 7 is from Plinta (1989):

1. what it needs
2. what it provides
3. what it does (not to be confused with how it does it)
4. performance documentation

5. rationale-type documentation
6. test software and documentation
7. adaptation description

Please see the papers for discussions of these items. We include some suggestions for Ada code component documentation in Appendix B. The *STARS Reusability Guidebook* (Wald 1986) suggests the following documentation to accompany a submittal to a library.

PART DESCRIPTION: title, type of component (code, design, etc.), type of function, purpose of function, interface requirements (include required information about the software and hardware not included with the component)

SUBMITTER DATA: name, address/network address, phone, contact

COMPONENT CONSTITUENTS: abstract, requirement specification, functional specification, design, algorithm or function, source code, object code, test specification, test code, test data/results, maintenance/operations (user's manual(s)), training materials

COMPONENT HISTORY: reason for component development, date of completion, description of applications used, frequency of use, description of development standards, version number

COMPONENT RELATIONSHIPS: name of parent, name of children, name and version of siblings, used by, uses

COMPONENT ATTRIBUTES: keywords (to search/retrieve on), development language, host environment (computer and operating system), target environment (computer and operating system)

RESTRICTIONS: government, developer, environment imposed (e.g., compiler, tools, peripherals), reusability metrics

DISCLAIMERS: warnings, problems, limitations, lack of tests

SOFTWARE SUPPORT: support organization or person, qualification, frequency of update

MISCELLANEOUS INSTRUCTIONS: how to get part, fees, warranties

RELEASES: transfer and/or assignment of copyright, transfer of ownership of hard goods

DELIVERABLE MEDIA DESCRIPTION: media, hard goods in delivery

MEDIA: electronic, magnetic, optical, paper, type of format (e.g., ASCII record, etc.)

As we have noted, code components should not be retained in the library without the corresponding designs, requirements, and test components. The relationships between them must either be explicitly stated (in the descriptions for the components) or be inherent in the library organization. Frakes and Nejmeh (1987) make specific suggestions about the form of structured comments to include with code, as do Chen and Ramamoorthy (1986). The structured-comments approach lends itself to automated extraction of the information fields for on-line retention in the library. The RSL system (Burton et al. 1987) employs this approach; we describe this system in detail in section 3.3.7. Biggerstaff (1989), of MCC, emphasizes the use of hypertext for depicting relationships and interconnecting available documentation for components.

Novak (1990) summarizes the technologies used so far in the development of library systems for reuse. They fall into the following three categories, with sub-categories as shown:

1. Information retrieval systems
   - Inverted index
   - Full text search
2. Database systems
   - Faceted classification
   - Taxonometric classification
   - Keyword search
3. Knowledge-based systems
   - Semantic description

He summarizes that the database has the strength of being well-understood, stable, and reliable, supporting relatively simple and inexpensive library techniques. On the other hand, databases may be too simple—i.e., unable to adequately represent the complex component interrelationships necessary for supporting large-scale software development. The knowledge-based approach can accommodate fine distinctions between components, but it will be expensive to amass the necessary knowledge, and it is unclear how well this technology will scale up for large-scale reuse.

We would add the observation that information retrieval techniques are especially attractive from the standpoint of library organization and entry of components into the library; with the full-text approach, no special structure or representation of component relationships would be necessary. It is, however, a largely-unexplored approach for software reuse libraries.

Novak (1990) comments that several library systems are moving towards commercial availability. These include the Westinghouse Reusability Search Expert (REUSE), the Eli system developed by NASA and Software Productivity Solutions, Inc., and the RCL developed by SofTech for ISEC.

We end the section with the following guidelines.

CC15: *Determine approach(es) for classifying and storing components, e.g., based on domain analysis.*

CC16: *Represent relationships between a component and its more (and less) abstract representations (as to life-cycle phase).*

CC17: *Represent relationships between a component and others that may collectively solve a given problem (or class of problems).*

CC18: *Represent relationships between components based on generalization/specialization.*

CC19: *Represent relationships between components based on decomposition (e.g., between a system specification and a subsystem specification).*

CC20: *Document each component thoroughly on-line, including user documentation and programming (i.e., maintenance) documentation.*

3.2.6 Case Study: A Design Study of Telephony Software at Ericsson Telecom

Oskarsson (1983) states that there are two ways to define the reusability of a software module:

- the tendency of its constituent parts to be reusable in unchanged form, or
- the possibility to reuse the complete module without changes.

The first definition would indicate that a module is reusable even if some modifications are required before reuse; the latter definition (which is the one Oskarsson chose for the study reported in this paper) indicates that reuse occurs when a module can be reused unchanged. As he notes, it is unreasonable to expect a module to be reused without changes if the concept it implements is changed.

In the study reported, the ability to reuse modules without changes was studied by isolating modules from each other through inability to share data and devices. Two modules are isolated from each other if they know little about each other's internals (Parnas 1972). It is generally assumed that the more a software module is isolated from other software, the more reusable it is. The concepts of data abstraction and object orientation attempt to achieve isolation by hiding the implementation of data structures—other modules can invoke operations on the data structure, but cannot access the data structure directly. However, the use of call-by-reference parameters may permit a called module to access the internal data structure of a calling module even though the calling module is object-oriented. What Oskarsson calls "extreme isolation" is the case when no data can be shared at all; i.e., not even call-by-reference is possible.

He believes that development of a new version of a software system is a good test of the reusability of the existing modules, since changes in functionality between system versions are similar to functional differences between different but related systems. When building a new system employing modules from a different system's architecture, one could expect to encounter more difficult reusability problems than when reusing modules between system versions. Oskarsson contends, however, that software reusability is only feasible inside a specific architecture or class of architectures, so he believes reuse between system versions can tell us a great deal about reusability in general.

AXE, the software system on which this study was based, is a commercial system developed by Ericsson Telecom in Sweden for public telephone exchanges. AXE has gone through numerous modifications and extensions to cover new markets and new telephone functions. The system contains millions of source code lines in a high-level programming language, and more than 1000 programmers and analysts have been engaged in continuing software development.

AXE software modules have the following characteristics:

- No data is shared between modules (i.e., all data is local to some module). Thus data transfer between modules is achieved by call-by-value, meaning that input data is copied into the called module.
- Only one software module can directly communicate with a hardware device; thus hardware is local to a module in the same way that a data structure is local in the object orientation.
- A module can have several entry point names (each corresponding to an operation) and entry names can be duplicated

between modules; message addresses consist of module identity and entry point name.

- Communication between modules is asynchronous. A module continues execution after it sends a message, and called modules are not required to return control to the caller.
- All modules are regarded as equals. There is no hierarchy of modules, and during system operation there is only one copy of each module.
- All program code is contained within a module. There are no global subprograms.

AXE has the flavor of a network of isolated, relatively autonomous modules that communicate by messages. An activity in the system jumps around among various modules, executing an operation in each (a part of the program code, chosen by entry point). The modules are relatively large—more than 1000 executable high-level program statements each.

Oskarsson gives the following reasons for restriction to local data and message passing in AXE:

- The need for communication among designers of different modules is reduced.
- Program errors in one module cannot directly damage data in the rest of the system.
- Concurrency problems are simplified.

Oskarsson groups modules into three types depending on the main purpose of each: (a) data modules, (b) interface modules, and (c) activity modules. The data modules of AXE implement a data abstraction. Each such module in the system handles a large data structure and performs storages and retrievals for other modules by means of messages. In the reuse study reported by Oskarrson, there was no need to alter existing data structures except to extend them for added capability.

The interface modules of AXE handle communication with the environment of the software—subscribers, operators, hardware devices, etc. The modules can be viewed as abstractions of parts of the environment. The modules isolate the details of hardware, etc., from the rest of the system, promoting reusability. For modules of these types to be considered reusable, they should not need to be changed when the corresponding data structure, part of the environment, or activity is unchanged. The same system can work with a new environment by changing only the interface modules.

Each activity module controls some part of the system's behavior, sending requests to and receiving information from other modules. An activity module is therefore an abstraction of something the system does (e.g., setting up a call or supervising connections). The allocation of system functionality to modules is intended to require only small amounts of data to be sent between modules.

Oskarsson noted that a few changes were needed in interface modules to satisfy new requirements, even though the environment did not change. However, most new requirements had no impact on the interface modules. Changes in activities brought about alterations to some activity modules that were reused, and also resulted in a few activity modules not being reused because their functionality no longer corresponded to requirements.

Oskarsson cites two principal reasons for reusability in the AXE system, namely (a) handling module identities as data and (b) locality of data and devices. Regarding the first reason, a module has no built-in knowledge of any other module, per se; at run time a module's identity can be sent in a message as ordinary data. Thus a module can send its identity when communicating with another module, and the identity can be used for subsequent communication. A module could, for example, inform other modules about its existence at system startup, or parameters can be entered during setup to indicate what modules are present. Thus new modules can be entered without impacting existing modules at all. Also, a module with good reuse potential could be used in other applications without any indication its context had changed. Oskarsson gives two small examples to illustrate the benefits of treating module identity as data.

Oskarsson points out that most modern systems are designed to localize handling of hardware devices, thus the locality of devices in AXE is not as unusual as locality of data. The principle of data locality—having operations on data conducted by the module that contains the data structure—encourages designing modules with little intercommunication. This tends to make modules self-contained and mutually independent (i.e., they are characterized by low coupling, and presumably by high cohesion as well). In the AXE system two basic structures are used for module intercommunication: the star shape and the chain (i.e., sequence) of modules. The star is a cluster of modules in which one central module has control; the central module communicates with others in the star, routing requests and information among them. The other modules do not communicate directly among themselves. A chain of modules passes control back and forth within the chain. Stars and chains are put together to solve a problem; for example, a member of a chain could be the central module in a star cluster with support service modules. Oskarsson states that the backbone of the AXE software structure consists of a few stars and chains of modules. This approach of limiting the variability of the software architecture is intended to reduce system complexity, and is guided by rules and common practice. Oskarsson notes that this amounts to reuse of the basic software architecture, which is something different than the reuse of individual modules.

Oskarsson cites a disadvantage to the relative isolation of modules, in that if a new requirement causes the need for a given module to obtain data from a module with which it previously had no direct communication, it must either send messages through intermediate modules, or obtain the module's identity after the first data access and communicate directly with it after that. The former approach implies modifying the intermediate modules to forward the message. While this is undesirable, it is preferable to the latter approach, which would give rise to an undisciplined intercommunication arrangement among modules. This same problem might arise in a hierarchical structure of subroutines. A disadvantage of localizing data access to a single module is that the management of multiple sets of data may result in multiple modules in which there is considerable duplication of functionality. The alternative to this—combining the data sets together under control of a single module—would be unacceptable due to the high communication load and resulting bottleneck that would characterize the new module. While such disadvantages may arise, they would likely not be sufficiently troublesome to offset the benefits to be gained from the module isolation/locality-of-data approach.

Oskarsson goes through the details of how new requirements impacted existing modules and assesses why module changes were necessary. His conclusion is that the approach of extreme isolation of modules has important advantages in terms of potential reuse of modules without change. The approach can accommodate modules that are "plug-in units" that can be replaced to adapt to new needs or changing environments, with no impact on surrounding modules (i.e., the surrounding modules can be reused).

Oskarsson emphasizes that module interfaces must be small, since message passing is expensive in terms of program code and processor load. The recommended approach is to have modules that are good abstractions; i.e., have modules that implement completely a well-defined concept and nothing else. The combination of good abstractions and handling module identities as data strongly contribute to reuse of both modules and system architecture, according to Oskarsson.

A final point worth emphasizing is that such characteristics as module isolation can contribute to reuse if and only if the concept abstracted by a module is needed in later systems. This understanding must provide guidance during decomposition of the system into modules, if reuse is to be encouraged.

3.3 Reusing Components

A number of operational issues must be satisfactorily addressed to effectively make use of available reusable components. Included are (a) classifying and storing components (which we considered in section 3.2.5), (b) identifying components that meet specific needs, (c) understanding identified components, (d) adapting components as necessary, and (e) assembling components into a complete software system. We consider issues (b) through (e) here. In Section 3.3.1 we discuss the important issue of cognitive aspects of reuse. Section 3.3.6 discusses a study assessing the characteristics of components and the extent of their of reuse. The study is based on successful software reuse activities at GSFC. Section 3.3.7 presents a detailed discussion of the Reusable Software Library (RSL) at Intermetrics, Inc. This system seeks to address all the operational issues listed.

3.3.1 Cognitive Aspects

Curtis (1989) has examined some issues of software reuse from a cognitive standpoint. Curtis stresses that programmers reuse knowledge they already possess each time they undertake a software development task, and that in fact the hallmark of professionals is their ability to reuse knowledge and experience to perform their tasks ever more efficiently. He believes that, among the difficulties in reusing software artifacts, there are three limitations stemming from cognitive processes.

- Programmers often try to force the application requirements to fit a structure for which they know a solution, even if it fails to satisfy some of the original specifications.
- The solutions that programmers know to problems in one domain may not transfer to problems in another domain.
- The form in which a problem statement is presented to programmers may disguise cues in the structure of the problem or the solution that would trigger recognition of potentially reusable artifacts.

The fact that programmers often know little about a particular application area further compounds the difficulty.

Our short-term memories are very limited in capacity—usually assumed to hold only about seven items of information. Curtis notes that we overcome this limitation by "chunking" information into units;

recalling a unit serves as a cue to recall all the information associated with it. An example given by Curtis is that the label "array sum" can become a chunk representing a code fragment for computing the sum of a sequence of elements. As Curtis observes, "array sum" takes up far less of the limited short-term memory space than the full code fragment, and it can trigger recall of all the fragment content when needed. High-level programming languages employ this principle in allowing a programmer to write a single high-level statement that may result in many machine language instructions. The approach of chunking is to hide a low-level procedural implementation under a higher-level concept. Applying the concept of chunking, reuse of components will be facilitated if a programmer can label the component's function as an easily recognized concept.

Curtis cites studies which demonstrated that programmers with greater experience decomposed a problem more fully into minimally interacting parts, and that they terminate the decomposition process for a particular aspect of the problem when it has been decomposed to a level at which a known solution pattern can be retrieved. It is very important to approach reuse in such a way as to take advantage of what is known about human cognitive processes. Curtis notes that a programmer must (a) comprehend the customer's requirements and the specification in order to make judgments about the suitability of available components; (b) be aware of the existence of specific relevant components; (c) be able to determine how well a candidate component matches the required functional specification (implying comprehension of the component's functional behavior); and (d) be able to comprehend the computational structure of the component if it is to be modified.

Curtis points out that in order for programmers to make the best use of a reusable library, they must be able to determine quickly what is available. He emphasizes the importance of organizing information in ways that reflect the user's mental model of the domain—i.e., having an indexing scheme similar to the knowledge structures possessed by most programmers working in an application area. He points out that the knowledge structures of inexperienced programmers are quite dissimilar, but that as programmers gain experience their understanding gravitates toward a common structure. Curtis thus concludes that, while a single organizational structure will not be suitable for all users, a generic structure can be found for a particular domain that will be increasingly effective for programmers as they gain experience; the generic structure sought is one closely resembling the organization of knowledge employed by experts in the application domain. Curtis comments on the need for interactive aids for library searches, but notes that interface and retrieval aids need to be flexible enough to serve both novice and expert users. He mentions that some features that would be helpful to a novice in conducting a library search could be redundant with knowledge structures an expert already possesses.

Curtis discusses various other issues pertaining to the experience level of programmers who would undertake software reuse. With novices, having components to reuse is not the issue. Novices are faced with difficulties in correctly specifying what should be done in the first place, and in determining which, if any, available components correspond. Curtis advocates the use of a reuse library for educational purposes—e.g., having in the library previous designs for the application domain, with rationale behind design decisions, to help inform novices of crucial design issues in the domain. Curtis believes that novices can benefit by exploring existing artifacts and documentation just for the purpose of increasing understanding of solution strategies and becoming informed about what is available. Even experienced personnel can benefit by using reusable design templates and corresponding rationale.

Curtis cautions that intermediate programmers' partial knowledge of an application area may lead them to believe they have located an appropriate component just because it has the right title. And they may massage the specifications more than is warranted to fit a solution strategy they already understand and/or to use available reusable components. Such attempts must be assessed by an experienced supervisory programmer, and perhaps by the customer if the specifications as stated will not be met.

3.3.2 Searching and Retrieving

In the case of the faceted classification scheme (Prieto-Diaz and Freeman 1987), the search is based on specification of a sextuple of descriptive keywords, or facets (see section 3.2.5). The user forms a query using the thesaurus to select a representative term for each facet. The user can use the asterisk rather than a keyword for a facet to generalize the query. The user can also request "expansion" of a query by having one of the specified facets replaced by other keywords, in order of conceptual closeness. The researchers have also attempted to provide ranking of the retrieved components based on user profiles; e.g., it is more important for novice programmers to attempt to use very small programs (in terms of lines of code) than is true for more experienced programmers.

Ramamoorthy, Garg, and Prakash (1986) have developed the Resource Extractor (REX) for use in forming queries using attributes and/or relations as qualifiers. Examples of their queries are

```
SET  High_Req = Software_Resources
     Classification = Requirements
     Performance = High.
```

This results in the creation of a set High_Req containing those elements of the set Software_Resources whose elements satisfy the specified relation and attribute.

Wood and Sommerville (1988) provide a forms-based interface to their library implementation on a SUN* workstation; it prompts the user for either a verb describing the action of a component or for a noun representing an object manipulated by the component. Thereby the system undertakes construction of a component-descriptor frame (section 3.2.5); partially completed frames are used to search the database; the user is provided lists of candidates for filling in other slots; and on-line helps are available. The user can select either a keyword search, in which an exact match on specified names must occur, or can permit components to be retrieved based on conceptual classes of verbs, for example. They plan to extend the system to include a browsing mode, and tools to integrate reuse with automated design tools.

Tarumi, Agusa, and Ohno (1988) have developed a rule-based retrieval mechanism based on user inputs of object names, attributes, relations, and operations. Names may have aliases. Their approach is a mixture of formal and informal methods; they emphasize the importance of this combination, believing that it yields simplicity and user friendliness.

Frakes and Nejmeh (1987) propose the use of IR systems for locating code components for reuse (and this could be extended to other abstraction levels). IR systems deal with formatted text, as well as unformatted text, which is not usually dealt with by database management systems. They have devised a novice user mode, which is menu driven, and a command mode for more experienced users. They have developed an experimental system called CATALOG, written in C under UNIX and MS-DOS. Help messages are available, and partial term matching is done using such sophisticated IR techniques as automatic stemming and phonetic matching. They propose that all components submitted to a reuse library must begin with a standard prologue of descriptive information, to form the basis for subsequent search and retrieval of the component (e.g., name, description, supporting documents, author, date, usage, parameters). With the advent of special-purpose hardware for IR (e.g., see Smith 1989) and resulting greatly improved responsiveness, IR techniques should be considered

---

* SUN is a registered trademark of SUN Microsystems, Inc.

as candidates for reuse library support. Frakes and Nejmeh (1987) also mention the promise of user feedback in conjunction with IR use.

Three important aspects of the IR process are discussed by Wood and Sommerville (1988). They are recall, precision, and ranking. Recall pertains to the percentage of relevant components that are identified; precision pertains to the percentage of identified components that are relevant; and ranking orders identified components by quality of match (to address the "information overload" issue). These are all substantive issues and will be increasingly important as reuse libraries become larger.

Carstensen (1987) described an approach to library browsing in which the user may specify English language nouns and verbs as search vectors. Based on potential matches, the user is first presented two-sentence abstracts of all candidate components. If desired, a more complete abstract (up to one page in length) may be requested for any of the components.

Several of the retrieval approaches mentioned above emphasize user-friendly interfaces. Burton et al. (1987) discuss and depict their approach to an interactive interface in their RSL system. This system is discussed in detail in section 3.3.7.

The ease of use of the reuse system is a very important issue, and it deserves special emphasis in planning for and implementing reuse within an organization. The following guidelines pertain to the above discussion.

RC1: *Devise and implement a mechanism for search and retrieval supporting query and browsing modes.*

RC2: *Emphasize user-friendly interface for search and retrieval.*

RC3: *Provide indication of "goodness of fit" of components to a query.*

3.3.3 Understanding and Assessing Components

Standish (1984) estimates that software maintenance accounts for 70 to 90 percent of the life cycle cost and that understanding accounts for 50 to 90 percent of maintenance cost. This would mean that understanding accounts for 35 to 80 percent of life-cycle cost. Understanding is absolutely critical to software reuse, especially if a component must be adapted.

Component understanding includes many aspects such as the creation of the component within the framework of a well-understood, consistent software engineering process (section 2.2) and good approaches to development, testing, and maintenance, as discussed in section 3.2. The existence of effective domain analysis information, and knowledge of how a component fits within the domain can be most helpful in understanding how the component may be used. In short, if good practices are followed in developing, classifying, and storing reusable components, thorough understanding should be a natural by-product.

Bott and Wallis (1988) argue that (a) we need to use components that implement fairly complicated functions to achieve large benefits from reuse and (b) to do so it is essential to reduce the perceived complexity of components as seen by the system designer. They maintain that, to this end, components must be designed for reuse from the beginning; their major theme is that components must conform to some kind of simplified "user model" of the system that they support, which will relieve the user of detailed coding concerns. An example of such a user model is that of compiler construction (the front-end/back-end division and the compiler phases). They also note that UNIX users benefit from the simplicity of its "user model"; although it is a very complicated system, enough can be learned very quickly to allow useful activities to occur. Biggerstaff and Richter (1987) refer to this simplified model as the "mental model" and state that developing such a model is probably the fundamental operational problem to solve in development of any reuse system. They suggest the use of hypertext to help solve the problem.

DeMillo, Du, and Stansifer (1989) at Purdue emphasize the use of operational history information in assessing candidate reusable components. They developed an experimental system to log some types of observations on component use, for query by a prospective user. They suggest the use of such experience information as security observations, extent of use, reported failures and faults, and performance observations (e.g., execution efficiency and memory utilization). Some of this data can be collected automatically, while some must be supplied explicitly by users. The importance of accumulating such usage data should be stressed, and an organization should implement procedures to acquire the necessary feedback.

We often face the need to understand and seek to reuse existing software that was not developed for reuse. In addition the existing software may not be well understood by the prospective reusers (nor perhaps by anyone available to the prospective reusers). Some approaches are discussed here for dealing with this issue. Chen and Ramamoorthy (1986) have developed the C Information Abstractor, which scans C programs and stores information into a database. The information obtained primarily relates to objects that can be accessed across C file or function boundaries—namely files, functions, global variables, global types, and macros. An Information Viewer provided to operate on the database provides answers to such questions as what functions call a given function, where a certain variable is defined, what functions access a given global variable, and what is the variable type. Since some important information cannot be extracted from the code (e.g., underlying assumptions, the algorithm used, computational complexity, and the necessary preconditions), Chen and Ramamoorthy propose the use of structured comments to provide the information to the abstractor. Examples of such information they suggest are purpose, assumptions, preconditions, assertions, algorithm description, and algorithm complexity.

Chen and Ramamoorthy (1986) also comment on software metrics, noting that software quality, testing required, and maintainability depend on such metrics as function-to-file bindings, file-to-file bindings, the number of objects related to a given function, and the number and depth of calling paths starting from a function. They observe that an examination of such metrics may well indicate the need for restructuring prior to reuse. They are considering means to handle some of the details automatically using the program database.

"Reverse engineering"—approaches for "unraveling the product ...to its earlier life cycle development phase(s)" (Sayani 1987)—can provide important leverage in aiding the understanding process and alleviating to some extent the need to attempt to understand code. Biggerstaff (1989) describes work at MCC in reverse engineering by providing a good overview of their reverse engineering system (Desire Version 1.0) and summarizing other commercially available reverse engineering tools. Desire operates within the framework of an object-oriented domain model and consists of a parser, a set of postprocessing functions, and the PlaneText hypertext system for use in presentation. There is considerable use of informal knowledge in their process, as a human user interacts with and guides the process.

Now we offer summary guidelines for this section.

RC4: *Seek to facilitate understandability of reusable components through effective domain analysis, good software development practices, and good classification and storage mechanisms.*

RC5: *Seek approaches/tools to help understand software not specifically prepared for reuse (e.g., reverse engineering).*

RC6: *Use operational history of components in assessing their suitability for reuse.*

RC7: *Obtain feedback from users of components, including number of uses, degree of satisfaction, and errors.*

3.3.4 Adapting Components

The ideal situation is that a component (or components) will be identified that exactly meets the need. That will often not be the case, however. Understanding the component (section 3.3.3) is the key to the decision process. "Goodness of fit" of an available component might well be measured by the effort required for adaptation. This would provide guidance when multiple components are identified that are candidates for selection. If a code component's functionality, accuracy, and execution time are adequate—i.e., it performs a needed role in an acceptable way—there should be little or no adaptation required provided that the component is highly cohesive and has no side effects.

If code requires adaptation, the design and/or specifications corresponding to the code component (and hopefully retained in the library) will likely prove to be very important. If the component must be rewritten in a different programming language, the high level design should serve as the basis—which is also true if the number of code "patches" required for adaptation is large. It is apparent that a high-level design should be easier to adapt than code and that a specification is more general and more adaptable than a design.

Ramamoorthy, Garg, and Prakash (1986) suggest some parameters for use in deciding whether to reuse a component. They are

$DesQ$	design quality;
Dev	availability of the original developers;
$DocQ$	documentation quality;
$Emal$	effort the organization needs for maintaining a line;
Eml	effort the organization predicts for modifying a line;
Enl	effort the organization needs for writing a new line;
Exp	experience with the package to be reused;
M	match for nonfunctional characteristics;
Nel	number of errors found per fixed number of lines;
Net	number of errors found in some fixed period;
Nmr	number of lines to be modified for reuse;
Nnr	number of lines to be written if no reuse;
Nr	number of lines that are being reused;
Nrb	number of times previously reused;
Org	organization maintaining the package to be reused;
$Time$	time available for the project.

Some suggestions for deciding which component to reuse are

1. The inequality $Nmr \times Eml < Nnr \times Enl$ should be true.
2. Net and Nel should be less than predefined constants.

3. *DocQ* and *DesQ* should be greater than some predefined minimum constants.
4. Make use of *Nrb*, *Net*, and *Nel* in assessing the quality of a candidate component.

Space limitations prohibit discussing these ideas in more detail here; they are included as a beginning point for considering such issues. The interested reader may see the referenced paper for more background and details.

Parameterized code is developed with the intent that input parameters cause "adaptation" of the code as pre-planned. And, generators are driven by input directives to "adapt" within a pre planned range. Ada generic procedures provide a mechanism for developing a "family" of procedures for which data types may be specified—and thus a specific "adaptation" created. It is very likely, at least in the near term, that most adaptation will be done manually. To that end, as suggested earlier, it will be extremely beneficial if the developers of a component will record suggestions for adapting the component for somewhat different uses.

Basili et al. (1989) are undertaking research to evaluate the reuse implications of Ada modules based on the explicit and implicit bindings of a module with its environment. They are experimenting with tools to assess the effort necessary to transform Ada code for reuse in different contexts.

Some research is addressing the desire to build "automatic adaptation" capability into code. Two examples of such research follow. Asdjodi has developed, as part of a prototype reuse system, the capability to automatically alter data structures as required for use by a selected component; thus, for example, if the output of one component is a matrix and the input for another is a linked list, her knowledge-based system would cause automatic generation of the required linked list (Asdjodi 1988; Asdjodi and Hooper 1989). In the prototype system only matrices and linked lists are used; however, the concepts could be extended to any type of data structures. She devised the very high-level language ELL as a means for specifying components to be composed; the user is thus shielded from many details.

Notkin and Griswold (1988) have developed a UNIX-based "extension" mechanism, based on an Extension Interpreter (EI). The EI consists of an arbitrator, which hierarchically maps procedure names to procedure implementations; the dynamic linker, which gives the flavor of interpretive environments like LISP; and the translation subsystem, which translates data between representations used by different languages. These components connect program components with a user interface. Their emphasis is on reusing source code without the

need to change it. Thus, the more fine-grained the available procedures, the more likely that new capabilities can make use of them.
The following guidelines are provided.

> **RC8:** *Use higher-abstraction representations in adapting a com-
> ponent (e.g., use design when adapting code).*

> **RC9:** *Emphasize the use of available metrics/tools to assess
> adaptation effort.*

> **RC10:** *Conduct testing of resulting code components relative to
> intended application environments.*

3.3.5 Composition of Code Components

"Composition" refers to interconnecting components to form software systems. The most straightforward approach may be used when
the component is a procedure that perfectly meets the need; then
composition results from a procedure call, coupled with the action of
the "linker." The same is true, of course, if we can successfully adapt a
procedure. This is at present the primary mechanism for composition.

Other important mechanisms for composition are UNIX pipes and
inheritance in object-oriented languages. Both of these have considerable benefit in shielding the user from the need to understand code,
per se; in the best case the code can be treated as a "black box."

Tracz (1987) describes a reuse system based on Ada components,
using both parameterization and application generators. He describes
an interactive dialogue of menus and prompts to obtain necessary parameters for a particular application. Then, based on the component
library and the parameters, the generator creates a compilable Ada
application program. To prepare for reuse in a given application domain, it is necessary to do a domain analysis (discussed in section
3.1), identifying likely candidate applications. Parameterizing must
be done, ranging from something as simple as character strings that
may be substituted in the source code, to specification of how to assemble pieces of a program. In the latter case, it could be that an
existing program was "dissected" for just this purpose as a result of
domain analysis.

Goguen (1986) proposes to achieve composition by means of the
"Library Interconnection Language" (LIL). As it stands, LIL's syntax
is Ada-like and relies on Goguen's earlier work based on specification
by use of axioms. He lists the following desirable techniques for constructing new entities from old ones:

1. Set a constant (e.g., the maximum depth of a stack).

2. Substitute one entity for a stub or parameter in another.
3. Sew together two entities along a common interface.
4. Instantiate the parameters of a generic entity.
5. Enrich an existing entity with some new features.
6. Hide (abstract or encapsulate) some features of an existing entity, either data or control abstraction.
7. Slice an entity to eliminate unwanted functionality.
8. Implement one abstract entity using features provided by others (leading to the notion of a vertical hierarchy of entities).

LIL is an example of a module interconnection language. The goal of such languages is to interconnect modules—which may be written in different programming languages—without having to modify the modules, assuming that they provide needed functionality.

Asdjodi devised an approach for high-level code component composition based on the use of a very high language ELL (Asdjodi 1988; Asdjodi and Hooper 1989). From an ELL input, supplying the name and parameters for available library modules, the modules are instantiated and written to a text file, with necessary declarations, for compilation and execution. The user is thus spared much detailed, error-prone work.

In section 3.2.2.2 the object-oriented MELD mechanism of Kaiser and Garlan (1987) is discussed. The idea is to compose object-oriented components by merging data structures and methods from different components.

The following guidelines ensue from the discussion of this section.

RC11: *Use existing mechanisms for composition to the extent practical (e.g., procedure linking, UNIX pipes, inheritance in object-oriented languages, etc.)*

RC12: *Seek automated approaches to composition as understanding permits.*

RC13: *Conduct integration testing as composition is achieved.*

3.3.6 Case Study: A Quantitative Study of Spacecraft Control Software Reuse at GSFC

Selby (1989) provides insights into effective approaches for achieving software reuse by providing a very detailed study and analysis of empirical data from one particular setting in which software reuse is successfully practiced. The organization is GSFC, and the application area is ground support software for unmanned spacecraft control. Selby studied 25 software projects of moderate to large size conducted at GSFC. The systems ranged in size from 3000 to 112,000 lines of Fortran source code; they took between 5 and 140 person-months to develop over a period of 5 to 25 months, with staff size ranging from 4 to 23 persons per project. There were from 22 to 853 modules in each system. "Modules" refers to the subroutines, utility functions, main programs, macros, and block data in the systems. In these 25 systems, the amount of software either reused or modified from previous systems averaged 32 percent per project.

Selby intended in his analysis to answer the following questions:

- How can reusable software be characterized?
- At what level (project, subsystem, or module) can software be reused most effectively?
- How does the extent of software reuse (e.g., complete reuse, slight modification, or extensive modification) affect the software development effort?
- How do the interface characteristics of a software component affect its frequency of reuse?
- How can reused software be characterized in terms of revision history, development effort, and static attributes such as size and control-flow information?
- How does project scale affect the amount of reused software?
- How can the proportion of development effort spent in design, implementation, test, and overhead be characterized when modules are newly developed, modified from previous systems, or reused without change?

Selby employed statistical techniques and statistical software packages to examine interrelationships of various factors pertaining to design and development of software. He considered:

1. module origin
    - complete reuse without revision
    - reuse with slight revision (less than 25 percent changes)
    - reuse with major revision (greater than or equal to 25 percent changes)
    - completely new development
2. module size
    - large (greater than 140 source lines)
    - small (less than or equal to 140 source lines)
3. project size
    - large (over 20,000 source lines)
    - small (under 20,000 source lines)

Selby also considered project start date (before September 1979 or September 1979 or later). However, data analysis relative to project size/date was inconclusive, except for one determination: projects of large size had a higher percentage of modules that were reused with major revision.

Aspects of module design and module implementation were also considered relative to reuse. Aspects of module design considered were

- interfaces that a module has with other system modules;
- interfaces that other system modules have with a module;
- interfaces that a module has with human users;
- documentation describing the functionality of a module;
- effort spent in designing a module.

Aspects of software implementation considered were

- changes in a module;
- control-flow structure in a module;
- assignment statements ("noncontrol flow structure") in a module.

Selby provides detailed statistical analysis of each of the aspects given above for both design and implementation. We provide a summary of his overall conclusions, and the interested reader can consult the paper for further details.

Module Design Characteristics. When compared with modules that were newly developed, extensively revised, or slightly revised, modules that were completely reused without revision had

- less interaction with other system modules in terms of the number of module calls per source line;
- simpler interfaces in terms of the number of input-output parameters per source line;
- less interaction with human users in terms of the number of read-write statements per source line;
- higher ratios of commentary to eventual implementation size in terms of the number of comments per source line.

When compared with newly developed modules, modules that were completely reused without revision had

- more interaction with utility functions in terms of the number of utility function calls per source line;
- a lower percentage of development effort spent on design (in the project in which the module was reused).

Module Implementation Characteristics. When compared with modules that were newly developed, extensively revised, or slightly revised, modules that were completely reused without revision had

- a smaller size in terms of the number of source lines;
- less total development effort in terms of the number of either total development hours or total development hours per source line;
- fewer changes in terms of the number of versions per source line.

When compared with newly developed modules, modules that were completely reused without revision had more assignment statements in terms of the number of assignment statements per source line.

Selby provides some comments concerning interpretation of the empirical results. He observes that completely reused modules tended to be (a) small, (b) well-documented, (c) equipped with simple interfaces; (d) characterized by little input-output (from/to other modules or human users); (e) "terminal nodes" in invocation hierarchies (when compared with newly-developed modules they had less interaction with other systems modules but more interaction with utility functions); (f) a product of little development effort or changes and a lower proportion of development effort spent in design activities (since likely only a walkthrough of an existing design was necessary, as compared to creating and assessing a new design); and (g) implementations of a sequential, as opposed to branching, nature due to their higher proportion of assignment statements.

Selby's interpretation of the finding that the larger projects had a greater percentage of reuse with major revisions reflects that developers, when working on large projects, may have greater motivation to reuse modules because of the project size.

Selby cautions about concluding causality of effects given some of the statistically significant relationships summarized above. For example, given that there is statistical significance between fewer input-output parameters and module reuse without revision, Selby is hesitant about assuming that simpler interfaces led to reuse of modules. He points out that in some cases causes and effects may not be cleanly separable from one another and from other factors affecting projects.

Selby characterizes software reuse as a natural process in the GSFC environment; it is by developer choice and not by management directive—thus the developers must be convinced of its payoff. There is also relatively low turnover of development personnel. There is variation in project functionality, yet the overall domain for all the projects is ground support software for unmanned spacecraft control, for which there is an established set of algorithms and processing methods. Thus reuse is facilitated by experienced personnel working in a stable, mature application domain.

At the time Selby's paper was written no automated tools were available to assist in the reuse process, but the development of an automated system was underway. Selby emphasizes the importance of reusing design information in addition to code and says this is a continuing theme in ongoing studies. Further analysis of the software discussed here is underway, based on additional project and module attributes, including information about software errors that occurred during development. Also, project data about reuse in another development organization will be analyzed.

3.3.7 Case Study: The Reusable Software Library (RSL) at Intermetrics, Inc.

Burton et al. (1987) describe work at Intermetrics, Inc. to provide tools and a methodology for reuse. They have developed prototype versions of the RSL and SoftCAD, a graphical design and documentation tool integrated with the RSL prototype. They have also developed tools to help librarians manage the database.

Their approach has been to plan a phased, long-term development to result in a reuse library to support large software development projects. They are prototyping the system in parts, and evaluating it as they proceed. They have planned seven phases as follows:

1. Analysis and requirements: identify characteristics of previous software libraries; identify classification scheme.
2. Develop initial RSL: design and implement prototype library; catalog initial holdings; provide capability for component evaluation.
3. Develop initial reuse-oriented design tool: develop interface to the library; provide support for OOD tool; support inclusion of reuse components into top-level design; support automatic generation of Ada program design language (PDL).
4. Integrate subsystems of the RSL: develop uniform user interface; migrate all subsystems of the RSL to a common window-oriented workstation.
5. Add additional functionality to the Reusable Software Library: add tools to support component entry.
6. Distribute Reusable Software Library: provide the capability of accessing the database from multiple machines across a sin-

gle company; provide support for multiple databases within a single company.

7. Formulate a Reusable Software Library for use by multiple companies: develop a RSL which can be tailored for the needs of many companies.

They first developed a software catalog with tools for component evaluation and reuse-oriented design. At the time of Burton's paper, the first three phases were complete and the fourth was underway.

The RSL consists of the database and four subsystems:

- Library Management
- User Query
- Software Component Retrieval and Evaluation (Score)
- Software Computer-Aided Design (SoftCAD)

The database is accessible to all subsystems, but can be modified only by the library management subsystem. Burton et al. are emphasizing Ada for developing reusable components because Intermetrics is engaged in many Ada-related activities and because of the promise of Ada's package and generic features for reuse. However, components written in any language may be entered into the library. Library components include functions, procedures, packages, and programs. Attributes are maintained in the database for all library components. The RSL librarian evaluates components to determine their reusability before accepting them and entering them into the library. Factors considered include a component's structure, functionality, complexity, level of testing, and quality of documentation, among others.

The developers of RSL have integrated the prototype tools into the software development life cycle. They portray the traditional life cycle as consisting of

- software requirements
- high-level software architecture
- design
- source code
- testing

They have integrated their tools into the design and coding phases. Using SoftCAD, a top-level design may be specified by means of object-oriented graphs and Ada PDL. The PDL may be used as a template to produce the detailed design and finally the source code. Reusable components may be accessed during both the design and coding phases. Software documents are generated automatically by processing the PDL or source code with an Ada-based PDL analyzer such as Intermetrics' Byron PDL analyzer. They anticipate savings in software verification if changes are not made to reused code, since each RSL component has undergone testing as a condition of library entry.

The Library Management subsystem provides tools for use by the librarian and quality-assurance personnel. Functions provided are for extracting reuse information from design or source code files, assuring the quality of candidate components, entering qualified components into the RSL database, and maintaining the database. Tools have been developed to

- automate data collection,
- standardize data entries,
- ensure continuity and consistency of reuse information across the life cycle,
- ensure completeness and reasonableness of reuse information, and
- provide for examination of reuse information.

Burton et al. developed a program to scan specially-labeled comment statements in PDL and source code files and to extract attributes. This data can be reviewed as a basis for entering a component into the database. The attributes currently supported are: UNITNAME, CATEGORY CODE, MACHINE, COMPILER, KEYWORDS, AUTHOR, DATE CREATED, LAST UPDATE, VERSION, REQUIREMENTS, OVERVIEW, ERRORS, ALGORITHM, DOCUMENTATION AND TESTING. UNITNAME is simply the name of a procedure, package, or subroutine. CATEGORY CODE relates the component to an application domain. REQUIREMENTS lists such special requirements as other components that must be available. OVERVIEW is a brief textual description. ERRORS describes any error handling, including exceptions that may be raised. DOCUMENTATION AND TESTING describes available documentation and test cases. The development team originally determined more than 60 attributes for inclusion, based on the needs when all 7 phases are complete. However they chose the above list for use in the prototype, after considering the planned usage context. Other information such as parameters and calling conventions may be obtained from the source code.

The developers devised a classification strategy based on a combination of two alternate approaches. The first is achieved by use of the CATEGORY CODE, and is determined for a component by predetermined hierarchical structures for application domains. Their experimentation at present is based on the domain of data structures. Examples of categories mentioned by Burton et al. are common math functions, data structures, and sort and search routines. They state that this scheme's concept is similar to that used by ACM Computing Reviews and the IMSL library. The second mechanism permits keywords to be stored for each component. The keywords are independent from the category code. This supports overlapping topics (e.g., a package may have procedures with different categories of functionality) and can grow with a project's needs.

In addition to examining the extracted attributes, quality assurance personnel must manually examine a component for correctness and quality before entering its attributes into the database. If the component is to be entered into the RSL database, additional functional and qualitative data must be entered by the librarian for later use by the Score subsystem.

The User Query subsystem provides both menu-driven and natural-language mechanisms. The menu supports the specification of attributes for a component search, and the generation of reports about the attributes of retrieved components (ranging from minimal information to all attributes for a component). Burton et al. provide the following examples of natural-language statements that would be accepted by the prototype system:

```
I need a stack package.
Only display those that implement garbage collection.
When were they written, and what version are they?
```

Action would be taken on these sequentially. They also show the example of "stack" being misspelled as "stak", with the system interrogating the user: by "stak" do you mean "stack"? The authors say that they have not yet fully explored the natural-language approach, but have observed that it is easier to use than the menu approach, but is much slower (from a factor of five to ten times as long response time, depending on the complexity of a query). They believe more research can improve performance and provide a viable alternative to traditional database queries.

Burton et al. developed the Score subsystem to ease the user's task of evaluating the "closeness of fit" of a component to the need. Their opinion is that a user would be overwhelmed at the prospect of manually evaluating and comparing all retrieved components. The approach of Score is based on application domains; the idea is that the significance of functional and qualitative attributes vary by domain. Functional attributes describe what a component does and how it is implemented. Qualitative attributes provide metrics that rate the quality of components; included are objective metrics such as line counts and complexity measurements, and subjective metrics such as readability, program structure, programming style, documentation and testing. The authors emphasize the importance of consistent quality ratings in making accurate evaluations of components against a user's requirements. They state that standard metrics must be established for each qualitative attribute, and guidelines must be defined for uniform grading practices. They say that consistent quality ratings are especially important for the subjective metrics.

The user is prompted to specify the required application domain and to indicate the relative importance of attributes within the domain. A library search is made for candidate components, which are rated according to the user's relative weightings. The system prompts the user for input of the attribute weightings by means of "barometers" displayed on the screen (i.e., an elongated vertical rectangle for each attribute, permitting all or part of the rectangle to be darkened to show the desired degree of emphasis). An example is given in Burton et al. of "set" being chosen as the type of data structure sought, from a list including tree, graph, stack, set, matrix, list, and string. The user is presented a screen showing a "barometer" for 14 different attributes: `bounded`, `managed`, `tasked`, `operations`, `domain`, `language`, `testing`, `inline_doc`, `overvw_doc`, `extern_doc`, `complexity`, `reuse_ease`, `type`, and `base_type`. Under each barometer is an arrow pointing upward and an arrow pointing downward. The user clicks on an arrow to raise or lower the importance of that attribute relative to the other attributes. In the example in the paper, the user raised the `operations` level to about 50 percent height, `language` to 100 percent, `testing` to about 20 percent, `overvw doc` to about 80 percent, `extern_doc` to about 40 percent, and `type` to 100 percent. These settings then gave rise to questions for the user; for example, since operations was stressed as being relatively important, the user was interrogated as to what operations were desired. Based on those listed, the user chose `difference`, `union`, `num_elements`, `is_proper_subset`, `is_subset`, `delete`, `insert`, and `is_member`. Based on this input, the system made a search and returned two candidates: `bounded_set_with_iterator` and `bounded_set`. They were listed in that order, with the first being recommended ahead of the other. The user was then at liberty to readjust the barometer levels, and make another search. This what-if process could continue until the user has adequately assessed available components.

The authors mention that, while this is a potentially powerful concept, there is the need for the attributes to be rated by personnel with software engineering expertise, and the rating method must be rigorously defined to have consistent ratings throughout the library. Also, their investigation was based on the class of data structures, for which the attributes are well defined, and determining the questions to ask was not as difficult as it would likely be for more complex domains. The authors have identified several desirable enhancements, including provision of a thesaurus to help relate similar attributes; defining uniform interfaces (e.g., parameters) for components in an application domain to facilitate both manual and automated component comparison and evaluation; and expanding the selection criteria to include more information about the environment where the desired component would be used (which could include the application area, a list of other components being reused, and a list of components being custom-designed for the application).

SoftCAD is a graphical design and documentation tool. It has been integrated with the RSL prototype to help in the high-level design of software. A designer can develop an architecture design by drawing OOD diagrams (as described in Booch 1987b), which are translated by SoftCAD into Ada PDL. Due to the integration of Soft-CAD with the RSL database, components already in the database can be included in a SoftCAD design and new components resulting from a SoftCAD design can be entered into the database. Burton et al. recommend drafting a rough OOD before beginning a session with SoftCAD and suggest that the designer be flexible about the design so that reusable components can be used if they closely match the need.

In Burton et al. 1987, SoftCAD screens are presented for a sample session. The first screen shows the top-level menu and a graphical depiction of the current design (including components with names Generic_List, DB_Interface, Hashing_Fctn, and User_Interface). From the menu, Design is chosen, which brings up the SoftCAD/RSL screen to permit searching for a component. By use of this screen, the designer may specify the category code if it is known. Up to five keywords describing the desired component's functionality may be provided also. In the sample session, the designer did not enter a category code, but entered the two keywords "String" and "Comparison" (up to five keywords may be specified). The search identified several candidate components, which the designer may examine with an on-line browsing capability. In the sample session, a package named String_Comparison was selected for inclusion in the design. To achieve inclusion of a reusable package, the designer indicates where placement should occur on the screen, indicates which subprograms are needed from the package, and draws connecting lines to indicate visibility and invocations of the package's subprograms. Finally, the generated Ada PDL was displayed. The usual approach is not to include the PDL of reused components in the PDL listing, but rather to indicate with in-line comments the component's name and where a machine-processable form of it can be found. Of course, if a component is to be modified its PDL would be included directly.

Burton et al. mention a number of planned enhancements. They plan to integrate a configuration management tool, with the capability to manage different versions of a component and to maintain information on the number of uses of a component and the success achieved. Because of the origins of different off-the-shelf software used in the system, it was originally distributed across an IBM PC and a VAX 11/750. They stated the intention to host all software on an IBM PC with a common-window operating environment. They planned to prompt for reuse comments to be included with generated PDL, for inclusion in the database. They also planned to develop the capability to generate OOD diagrams for existing components.

Other enhancements being considered included tools to help the librarian provide the necessary functional and qualitative attributes and to help determine an appropriate category code based on a component's characteristics. Further investigation of software metrics was underway. Also, they planned to solicit on-line comments from users on desirable improvements to meet their needs.

Burton et al. summarize some lessons learned from their work. As is true for every successful reuse project reported in this book, they mention that management must be actively involved in the reuse effort. They mentioned that Intermetrics' management had emphasized software reuse in the development of test and analysis tools written in Ada and designed to support Ada software development. As a result more than 33 percent of the delivered code was made up of reused packages. A problem at first was that several tools had poor performance due to the general nature of the reused code. However, they used a performance analyzer and tailored the code for the new application, which substantially improved performance.

They state as a significant outcome of this software development project the fact that management was able to achieve greater productivity by viewing software development as the production of a long-lived corporate asset rather than as an effort required to produce the current deliverable.

The authors state that perhaps the most important lesson learned from the prototype was the benefit of integrating the passive RSL with active design tools like SoftCAD, creating a system useful in design and implementation. They anticipate that separating the single RSL into multiple databases of smaller size, each containing project-specific reusable components, should greatly enhance the RSL's performance.

3.4 Tools and Environments

Software reuse should be practiced as an integral activity within a software engineering process (section 2.2). Thus the tools and environments for software engineering are directly supportive of software reuse (including use and creation of reusable components). There are, however, some needs unique to the reuse process per se. The newness of software reuse means that there are few mature tools and environments created especially for software reuse. As far as is known, no commercially available system presently purports to cover all the requirements for software reuse.

Following the 1987 Minnowbrook Workshop (Goel and McGarry 1987), a report was written summarizing the work of the working groups (Agresti and McGarry 1988). Here we will briefly consider the findings of Working Group 3 (Tools and Environments for Software Reuse).

The working group participants determined the following six categories of reuse-related activities that need to be supported: domain analysis, development and refinement of reusable products, classification, searching, evaluation and assessment, and incorporation of reusable items. Of this list, the first three categories pertain to the creation of reusable components and the last three to component reuse. Clearly these tools are not all necessary to conduct software reuse, but are important as research goals to help automate the reuse process. We will consider their recommendations for the six categories, in order. Progress has been made in the maturity level of some of these tools since the time of the workshop—the maturity levels shown are those assigned by the working group.

1. Domain Analysis

    Key subactivities: knowledge extraction, identification of objects and operations, abstraction and relationships, classification and taxonomy, and domain languages and synthesis.

    Support tools: [Maturity characterization codes are M (mature), D (developed but unproven), and U (undeveloped).]
    - Knowledge extraction tools, such as expert system building tools (D)
    - Entity-relationship diagramming tools (D)
    - Object-oriented development tools (U)
    - Semantic clustering and automatic classification tools (U)
    - Computer-aided software engineering (CASE) tools (D)
    - Parsing tools (M)

2. Development and Refinement of Reusable Products

Key subactivities with supporting tools:
- Isolate replaceable features: object-oriented languages (D), historical data collection (M)
- Make products self-contained: dependency analyzers (e.g., cross-reference generators) (D); structure analyzers (D)
- Parameterize: software and language features such as table-driven software, macro expansion, preprocessors, and generics (D)
- Enrich (add features to a product to widen its range of application): object-oriented languages (D), configuration management tools to manage multiple versions of a product (M)
- Abstract and specialize: languages that support class hierarchies and inheritance (e.g., Smalltalk) (M)
- Test and validate (to mitigate risk in reuse —the not-invented-here syndrome): test coverage analyzers (M)
- Formally verify: verification environment (U)
- Assess quality: quality metrics (D), standards checkers (M)
- Restructure (for multilevel reusability): reusability metrics (U)

3. Classification

Approaches: controlled vocabulary (e.g., faceted classification approach), uncontrolled vocabulary (e.g., Frakes and Nejmeh 1987), and knowledge representation.

Support tools: context clarification tool (D), semantic closeness tool (D), thesaurus construction tool (D), Boolean IR system (D), vector space IR system (D), word processing tools (M), semantic net shell (D), frame shell (D), and rule-based expert system shell (D)

4. Searching

Alternative approaches and support tools:
- Natural language: CATALOG tool (Frakes and Nejmeh 1987) (D)
- Structured queries: CATALOG tool (Frakes and Nejmeh 1987) (D)
- Browsing: Hypertext (D)
- Hierarchical: IMS, Smalltalk (D)
- Semantic search: Automated Library System (ALS) (D), SEMANTX (D)
- Citation search: Alicia (RADC) (D)

5. Evaluation and Assessment

Support tools: standard test sets (U), reuse-level measurement tools (U), attitude measurement tools (U), usage measurement tools (D), SMART environment (D)

6. Incorporation of Reusable Items

Subactivities and support tools:
- Selection of variants: source code difference tools (M)
- Instantiation: compilers (M)
- Provision of data: data generation (D), forms management (M)
- Template completion: prompters (M), macro expanders (M)
- Modification safety: maintenance support (M)
- Integration of items: linkers (M), smart editors (D), environments with integration paradigm (e.g., UNIX shell, Common Lisp, or Smalltalk) (M)

Please see Agresti and McGarry (1988) for references to the above items that are not included here. Some other tools have been mentioned in earlier sections of this book that are also important for reuse. Among them are cost modeling tools (Fairley et al. 1989), operational history recording/extraction tool (DeMillo, Du, and Stansifer 1989), Ada Data Binding Tool (Basili et al. 1989), and reverse engineering tools (e.g., Biggerstaff 1989). The RSL system is an example of an attempt to provide an environment for software reuse by integrating a number of tools together with a database of reusable components.

As was mentioned earlier, software reuse can be practiced without special tools, but it is important that the tools be developed—and they will no doubt be appearing over the next few years.

3.5 References

AdaIC (Ada Information Clearing House). June 1990. *Ada Information Clearinghouse Newsletter.* 8(2).

Agresti, W., and F. McGarry. March 1988. *The Minnowbrook Workshop on Software Reuse: A Summary Report.* NASA/GSFC, Greenbelt, Md., Computer Sciences Corporation, Beltsville, Md.

Arango, G. 1988. *Domain Engineering for Software Reuse.* Ph.D. dissertation, University of California, Irvine, Cal.

Asdjodi, M. 1988. *Knowledge-based Component Composition: An Approach to Software Reusability.* Ph.D. dissertation, The University of Alabama in Huntsville, Huntsville, Ala.

Asdjodi, M., and J. W. Hooper. June 1989. "An Environment for Software Reusability." In *Proceedings of the First International Conference on Software Engineering and Knowledge Engineering*, 48–53. Skokie, Ill.

Bailin, S. C. October 1987. "Informal Rigor: A Practical Approach to Software Reuse." In *Proceedings of the Workshop on Software Reuse*, ed. G. Booch and L. Williams. Rocky Mountain Inst. of Software Engineering, SEI, MCC, Software Productivity Consortium, Boulder, Colo.

Bailin, S. C. May 1989. "An Object-Oriented Requirements Specification Method." *Communications of the ACM* **32**(5), 608–23.

Bailin, S. C., and J. M. Moore. December 1987. "A Software Reuse Environment." In *Software Engineering Workshop*. NASA/GSFC, Greenbelt, Md.

Barsotti, G., and M. Wilkinson. March 1987. "Reusability–Not an Isolated Goal." In *Proceedings of the Conference on Software Reusability and Maintainability*, A1–A14. The National Institute for Software Quality and Productivity, Inc., Tysons Corner, Va.

Barstow, D. November 1985. "Domain-Specific Automatic Programming." *IEEE Trans. on Software Engr.*, **SE-11**(11), 1321–36.

Basili, V. R., and H. D. Rombach. December 1988. "Towards a Comprehensive Framework for Reuse: A Reuse-Enabling Software Evolution Environment." UMIACS-TR-88-92, University of Maryland, College Park, Md.

Basili, V. R., H. D. Rombach, J. Bailey, A. Delis, and F. Farhat. March 1989. "Ada Reuse Metrics." In *Guidelines Document for Ada Reuse and Metrics (Draft)*, ed. P. A. Lesslie, R. O. Chester, and M. F. Theofanos, 11–29. K/DSRD-54, Martin Marietta Energy Systems, Inc., Oak Ridge, Tenn., under contract to U.S. Army, AIRMICS.

Baxter, I. D. October 1987. "Reusing Design Histories via Transformational Systems." In *Proceedings of the Workshop on Software Reuse*, ed. G. Booch and L. Williams. Rocky Mountain Inst. of Software Engineering, SEI, MCC, Software Productivity Consortium, Boulder, Colo.

Bein, J., P. Drew, and R. King. March 1989. "Object-Oriented Data Base Tools to Support Software Engineering." In *Guidelines Document for Ada Reuse and Metrics (Draft)*, ed. P. A. Lesslie, R. O. Chester, and M. F. Theofanos, 95–110. K/DSRD-54, Martin Marietta Energy Systems, Inc., Oak Ridge, Tenn., under contract to U.S. Army, AIRMICS.

Biggerstaff, T. J. July 1989. "Design Recovery for Maintenance and Reuse." *Computer* **22**(7), 36–49.

Biggerstaff, T. J., and A. J. Perlis, ed. 1989a. *Software Reusability. Concepts and Models*, vol. I, ACM Press, Addison-Wesley, Reading, Mass.

Biggerstaff, T. J., and A. J. Perlis, ed. 1989b. *Software Reusability. Applications and Experience*, vol. II, ACM Press, Addison-Wesley, Reading, Mass.

Biggerstaff, T. J., and C. Richter. March 1987. "Reusability Framework, Assessment, and Directions." *IEEE Software Engr* **4**(2), 41–49.

Booch, G. 1987a. *Software Components with Ada.* Benjamin/ Cummings, Menlo Park, Calif.

Booch, G. 1987b. *Software Engineering With Ada*, 2nd ed. Benjamin/Cummings, Menlo Park, Calif.

Bott, M. F., and P. J. L. Wallis. 1988. "Ada and Software Re-use." *Software Engineering Journal* **3**(5), 177–83.

Braun, C. L., J. B. Goodenough, and R. S. Eaves. April 1985. *Ada Reusability Guidelines.* U.S. Air Force ESD 3285-2-208/2.1, SofTech.

Brooks, F. P. 1987. "No Silver Bullet: Essence and Accidents of Software Engineering." *IEEE Computer* **20**(4), 10–19.

Bullard, C. K., D. S. Guindi, W. B. Ligon, W. M. McCracken, and S. Rugaber. March 1989. "Verification and Validation of Reusable Ada Components." In *Guidelines Document for Ada Reuse and Metrics (Draft)*, ed. P. A. Lesslie, R. O. Chester, and M. F. Theofanos, 31–53. K/DSRD-54, Martin Marietta Energy Systems, Inc., Oak Ridge, Tenn., under contract to U.S. Army, AIRMICS.

Burton, B. A., R. W. Aragon, S. A. Bailey, K. D. Koehler, and L. A. Mayes. July 1987. "The Reusable Software Library." *IEEE Software* **4**(4), 25–33.

CAMP. 1987. "CAMP, Common Ada Missile Packages, Final Technical Report, Vols. 1, 2, and 3." AD-B-102654,-5,-6. Air Force Armament Laboratory, AFATL/FXG, Eglin AFB, Fla.

Carstensen, H. B., Jr. March 1987. "A Real Example of Reusing Ada Software." In *Proceedings of the Conference on Software Reusability and Maintainability*. The National Institute for Software Quality and Productivity, Inc., Tysons Corner, Va.

Cheatham, T. E. September 1984. "Reusability through Program Transformations." *IEEE Trans. on Software Engr* **SE10**(5), 589–594.

Chen, Y. F., and C. V. Ramamoorthy. October 1986. "The C Information Abstractor." In *Proceedings of Compsac 86*. Chicago.

Cleaveland, J. July 1988. "Building Application Generators." *IEEE Software* **5**(6), 25–33.

Cohen, J. July 1989. "GTE Software Reuse for Information Management Systems." In *Proceedings of the Reuse in Practice Workshop*, ed. J. Baldo and C. Braun. Software Engineering Institute, Pittsburgh, Penn.

Curtis, B. 1989. "Cognitive Issues in Reusing Software Artifacts." In *Software Reusability. Applications and Experience*, vol. II, Biggerstaff, T. J., and A. J. Perlis, 269-87. ACM Press, Addison-Wesley, Reading, Mass.

DeMillo, R. A., W. Du, and R. Stansifer. June 1989. "Reuse Oriented Ada Programming–A Prototype System," In *Proceedings of the Ada Reuse and Metrics Workshop*. Atlanta.

Deutsch, L. P. 1989. "Design Reuse and Frameworks in the Smalltalk-80 System." In *Software Reusability. Applications and Experience*, vol. II, Biggerstaff, T. J., and A. J. Perlis, 57–71. ACM Press, Addison- Wesley, Reading, Mass.

EVB Software Engineering, Inc. March 1987. "Creating Reusable Ada Software." In *Proceedings of the Conference on Software Reusability and Maintainability*, E1–E58.

Fairley, R., S. L. Pfleeger, T. Bollinger, A. Davis, A. J. Incorvaia, and B. Springsteen. 1989. *Final Report: Incentives for Reuse of Ada Components, vols. 1 through 5*. George Mason University, Fairfax, Va.

Frakes, W. B., and B. A. Nejmeh. January 1987. "Software Reuse through Information Retrieval." In *Proceedings of the Twentieth Hawaii International Conference on System Sciences*, ed. B. D. Shriver and R. H. Sprague, Jr., 530–35. Kailua-Kona, Hawaii.

Gagliano, R. A., M. D. Fraser, and G. S. Owen. March 1989. "Guidelines for Reusable Ada Library Tools." In *Guidelines Document for Ada Reuse and Metrics (Draft)*, ed. P. A. Lesslie, R. O. Chester, and M. F. Theofanos, 79–90. K/DSRD-54, Martin Marietta Energy Systems, Inc., Oak Ridge, Tenn., under contract to U.S. Army, AIRMICS.

Gautier, R. J. and P. J. L. Wallis. 1990. *Software Reuse with Ada.* Peter Peregrinus Ltd., London, U.K.

Goel, A. L. and F. McGarry. July 1987. *Proceedings of the Tenth Minnowbrook Workshop on Software Reuse*, Blue Mountain Lake, NY.

Goguen, J. A. February 1986. "Reusing and Interconnecting Software Components." *IEEE Computer* **19**(2), 16–28.

Guerrieri, E. March 1988. "Searching for Reusable Software Components with the Rapid Center Library System." In *Proceedings of the Sixth National Conference on Ada Technology*, 395–406. Arlington, Va.

Hartman, D. February 1989. "Rapid Prototyping Using Reuse." In *Reuse and the Software Revolution Symposium*. Falcon Air Force Base, Colo.

Hess, J. A., W. E. Novak, P. C. Carroll, S. G. Cohen, R. R. Holibaugh, K. C. Kang, and A. S. Peterson. June 1990. "A Domain Analysis Bibliography." CMU/SEI-90-SR-3.

Hooper, J. W. July 1988. "Simulation Model Reuse: Issues and Approaches." In *Proceedings of The 1988 Summer Computer Simulation Conference*, 51–56. Seattle.

Humphrey, W. S. June 1989. "The Software Engineering Process: Definition and Scope." *Software Engineering Notes* **14**(4), 82–83.

Horowitz, E., and J. B. Munson. September 1984. "An Expansive View of Reusable Software." *IEEE Trans. on Software Engr* **SE10**(5), 477–87.

Humphrey, W. S. June 1989. "The Software Engineering Process: Definition and Scope." *Software Engineering Notes* **14**(4), 82–83.

Hutchinson, J. W., and P. G. Hindley. 1988. "A Preliminary Study of Large-Scale Software Reuse." *Software Engineering Journal* **3**(5), 208–12.

ISEC (U.S. Army Information Systems Engineering Command). December 1985. *ISEC Reusability Guidelines.* U.S. Army Information Systems Engineering Command 3285-4-247/2, Softech Inc., Waltham, Mass.

Jette, C., and R. Smith. 1989. "Examples of Reusability in an Object-Oriented Programming Environment." In *Software Reusability, Vol. II, Concepts and Models*, ed. T. J. Biggerstaff and A. J. Perlis, 73–101. ACM Press, Addison-Wesley, Reading, Mass.

Kaiser, G. E., and D. Garlan. July 1987. "Melding Software Systems from Reusable Building Blocks." *IEEE Software* **4**(4), 17–24.

Kang, K. C. July 1989. "Features Analysis: An Approach to Domain Analysis." In *Proceedings of the Reuse in Practice Workshop*, ed. J. Baldo and C. Braun. Software Engineering Institute, Pittsburgh, Penn.

Lanergan, R. G., and C. A. Grasso. September 1984. "Software Engineering with Reusable Design and Code." *IEEE Trans. on Software Engr* **SE10**(5), 498–501.

Lee, K. J., and M. Rissman. July 1989. "Application of Domain-Specific Software Architectures to Aircraft Flight Simulators and Training Devices." In *Proceedings of the Reuse in Practice Workshop*, ed. J. Baldo and C. Braun. Software Engineering Institute, Pittsburgh, Penn.

Lieberherr, K. J., and A. J. Riel. April 1988. "Demeter: A Case Study of Software Growth through Parameterized Classes." In *Proceedings of the 10th International Conference on Software Engineering*, 254–64. Singapore.

Lubars, M. D. October 1987. "Wide-Spectrum Support for Software Reusability." In *Proceedings of the Workshop on Software Reuse*, ed. G. Booch and L. Williams. Rocky Mountain Inst. of Software Engineering, SEI, MCC, Software Productivity Consortium, Boulder, Colo.

Lubars, M. D. and M. T. Harandi. 1989. "Addressing Software Reuse Through Knowledge-Based Design." In *Software Reusability, Vol. II, Concepts and Models*, ed. T. J. Biggerstaff and A. J. Perlis, 345–77. ACM Press, Addison- Wesley, Reading, Mass.

Martin, J. 1985. *Fourth Generation Languages, Vol I, Principles.* Prentice-Hall, Englewood Cliffs, N.J.

McCain, R. October 1985. "Reusable Software Component Construction: A Product-Oriented Paradigm." In *Proceedings of the 5th AIAA/ACM/NASA/IEEE Computers in Aerospace Conference*, Long Beach, Cal., 125- -135.

McKay, C. W. March 1989. "Conceptual and Implementation Models." In *Guidelines Document for Ada Reuse and Metrics (Draft)*, ed. P. A. Lesslie, R. O. Chester, and M. F. Theofanos, 111–48. K/DSRD-54, Martin Marietta Energy Systems, Inc., Oak Ridge, Tenn., under contract to U.S. Army, AIRMICS.

McNicholl, D. G., C. Palmer, S. G. Cohen, W. H. Whitford, G. O. Goeke. 1986. *Common Ada Missile Packages (CAMP), Vol I: Overview and Commonality Study Results.* AFATL-TR-85-93, McDonnell Douglas, St. Louis.

Meyer, B. March 1987. "Reusability: The Case for Object-Oriented Design." *IEEE Software* 4(2), 50–64.

Mittermeir, R. T., and W. Rossak. October 1987. "Software Bases and Software Archives: Alternatives to Support Software Reuse." In *Proceedings of The 1987 Fall Joint Computer Conference*, 21–28. Dallas.

Neighbors, J. M. 1981. *Software Construction Using Components.* Ph.D. dissertation, University of California, Irvine, Cal.

Neighbors, J. M. September 1984. "The Draco Approach to Constructing Software from Reusable Components." *IEEE Trans. on Software Engr* **SE10**(5), 564–74.

Neighbors, J. M. October 1987. "Report on the Domain Analysis Working Group Session." In *Proceedings of the Workshop on Software Reuse*, ed. G. Booch and L. Williams. Rocky Mountain Inst. of Software Engineering, SEI, MCC, Software Productivity Consortium, Boulder, Colo.

Notkin, D., and W. G. Griswold. April 1988. "Extension and Software Development." In *Proceedings of the 10th International Conference on Software Engineering*, 274–83. Singapore.

Novak, W. E. June 1990. "U. S. Army SDS CRWG Reuse Committee Technical Requirements Document: Technical Guidance Section." (Preliminary Draft).

Oskarsson, O. 1983. "Reusability of Modules with Strictly Local Data and Devices." in *ITT Proceedings of the Workshop on Reusability in Programming.* Newport, R. I.

Palmer, C. July 1989. "Reuse in Practice." In *Proceedings of the Reuse in Practice Workshop,* ed. J. Baldo and C. Braun. Software Engineering Institute, Pittsburgh, Penn.

Parnas, D. L. 1972. "On the Criteria to be Used in Decomposing Systems into Modules." *Communications of the ACM* 15(12).

Plinta, C. July 1989. "A Model Solution for the C^3I Domain." In *Proceedings of the Reuse in Practice Workshop,* ed. J. Baldo and C. Braun. Software Engineering Institute, Pittsburgh, Penn.

Prieto Diaz, R. October 1987. "Domain Analysis for Reusability." In *Proceedings of Compsac 87,* 23–29. Tokyo.

Prieto-Diaz, R., April 1990. "Domain Analysis: An introduction." *ACM Software Eng. Notes* 15(2), 47–54.

Prieto-Diaz, R., and P. Freeman. January 1987. "Classifying Software for Reusability." *IEEE Software* 4(1), 6–16.

Ramamoorthy, C. V., V. Garg, and A. Prakash. October 1986. "Support for Reusability in Genesis." In *Proceedings of Compsac 86,* 299–305. Chicago.

Rice, J. G. 1981. *Build Program Technique: A Practical Approach for the development of Automatic Software Generation Systems.* Wiley, New York.

Rogerson, A. M., and S. C. Bailin. July 1987. "Software Reusability Environment Prototype: Experimental Approach." In *Proceedings of The Tenth Minnowbrook Workshop.* Software Reuse, Blue Mountain Lake, N.Y.

St. Dennis, R. J. May 1986. *A Guidebook for Writing Reusable Source Code in Ada (R), Version 1.1.* CSC-86-3:8213, Honeywell, Golden Valley, Minn.

St. Dennis, R. J. January 1987. "Reusable Ada Software Guidelines." In *Proceedings of the Twentieth Hawaii International Conference on System Sciences,* ed. B. D. Shriver and R. H. Sprague, Jr., 513–20. Kailua-Kona, Hawaii.

Sayani, H. March 1987. "Applications In Reverse Software Engineering." In *Proceedings of the Conference on Software Reusability and Maintainability,* ed. E. Yourdon, L1–L15. The National Institute for Software Quality and Productivity, Inc., Tysons Corner, Va.

SEI (Software Engineering Institute). June 1990. "Domain Analysis Project" (Briefing Charts presented by W.E. Novak at SDIO Reuse Committee Meeting, National Test Bed, Falcon AFB (Colorado Springs), CO).

Selby, R. W. 1989. "Quantitative Studies of Software Reuse," In *Software Reusability: Vol. II Applications and Experience*, ed. T. J. Biggerstaff and A. J. Perlis, 213-33.

Smith, S. R. 1989. *An Advanced Full-Text Information Retrieval System.* Ph.D. dissertation, The University of Alabama, Huntsville, Ala.

Soloway, E., and K. Ehrlich. September 1984. "Empirical Studies of Programming Knowledge." *IEEE Trans. on Software Eng.* **SE-10**(5).

Standish, T. A. September 1984. "An Essay on Software Reuse." *IEEE Trans. on Software Engr.* **SE10**(5), 494–97.

Tarumi, H., K. Agusa, and Y. Ohno. April 1988. "A Programming Environment Supporting Reuse of Object- Oriented Software." In *Proceedings of the 10th International Conference on Software Engineering*, 265–73. Singapore.

Tracz, W. January 1987. "RECIPE: A Reusable Software Paradigm." In *Proceedings of the Twentieth Hawaii International Conference on System Sciences*, ed. B. D. Shriver and R. H. Sprague, Jr., 546–55. Kailua-Kona, Hawaii.

Tracz, W. April 1990. "Where Does Reuse Start?" *ACM Software Eng. Notes* **15**(2), 42-46.

Van Scoy, R., and C. Plinta. July 1989. "An Informal Experiment in Reuse." In *Proceedings of the Reuse in Practice Workshop*, ed. J. Baldo and C. Braun. Software Engineering Institute, Pittsburgh, Penn.

Wald, E. 1986. *STARS Reusability Guidebook, V4.0* (Draft). U.S. Department of Defense, STARS.

Wegner, P. July 1984. "Capital-Intensive Software Technology." *IEEE Software* **1**(3).

Wood, M., and I. Sommerville. 1988. "An Information Retrieval System for Software Components." *Software Engineering Journal* **3**(5), 198–207.

Getting Started

4.1 Discussion

A software reuse program must provide significant economic benefit to
an organization to receive enthusiastic support—and even to survive.
Thus an organization should approach reuse in a pragmatic way. Sufficient commonality in current and anticipated software projects must
exist to justify investment in reuse (for staff training, library development, etc.). Thus the organization should assess one or more areas
of emphasis in which requirements for similar software frequently re-
cur. In the case of a corporation, a business decision should be made
whether to invest in a reuse program as an emphasis area. Whether
for a government organization or a corporation, the decision should
rest on present and expected requirements for recurring software; that
is, on predicting whether the benefit from reuse will be sufficient to
justify the investment.

In concert with the assessment of reuse potential, an organization
should identify its reusable assets. This could include commercially
available software with proven benefit to the organization as well as
internal software. The software identified can serve as an initial set of
components for reuse. Another very important asset for reuse is the
availability of professional personnel with knowledge and experience
in the area(s) of emphasis (i.e., domain experts).

Another important consideration in initiating a reuse program is
whether the organization is making use of effective software practices. It would be of little use to attempt a software reuse program
without having in place a systematic, consistent process for software
development and maintenance. SEI's process assessment procedure
(Humphrey et al. 1987) is the best-known instrument for such assessments; in the same vein, Fairley et al. (1989) have suggested a reuse
assessment instrument with a questionnaire based on the style of the
SEI assessment questionnaire. Shortcomings in the software process
should be remedied for the inherent benefit and to improve the basis
for reuse.

137

Before proceeding with a reuse program, it is critical that top-level management must be convinced of the worthiness of the undertaking. The economic analysis and assets assessment suggested should be an important factor in the management decision to proceed.

Having received top management's approval, at least to investigate the potential for reuse, a reasonable next step would be to undertake a pilot software project employing reuse. The project should be chosen very carefully, considering available domain expertise, existing software assets for the domain, and the likelihood that the project will benefit significantly from reuse. The pilot project will of necessity be based on near-term, comparatively well-understood requirements. If the results of the pilot project are encouraging, the project can lead to wider implementation of reuse practices within the organization. A phased, evolutionary approach can help develop needed reuse knowledge and skills as well as convince technical and managerial personnel of the viability of reuse. Integration of reuse into the organization's software process will be an important experimental activity of the pilot project; the process should be expected to evolve as additional experience is gained.

We have suggested numerous guidelines in earlier chapters, many of which pertain to a "steady state" reuse program in a sizable organization. Certainly not all of the guidelines are applicable to a pilot project (e.g., many of the organizational structure guidelines will not apply), to a small organization, or to a small segment of a larger organization.

As reuse experience builds, management must decide whether to propagate reuse practices to additional projects and organizational segments and the rate at which the propagation will occur. As reuse becomes more widespread, organizational procedures and policies should evolve, including a software engineering process incorporating the use and creation of reusable products and provisions for incentives for individuals and projects. The organizational infrastructure should be changed over time to support and foster reuse. It will be necessary from the very first pilot project to have a library of components (including, perhaps, some "pointers" to commercially available products not currently in the library).

The phased approach advocated here should involve considerably lower risk than trying to implement all aspects of a full-fledged reuse program immediately. The organization should continually assess the effectiveness of its reuse process, seeking to adjust as necessary to deal with problems encountered and to gain advantage from improved methods, tools, and policies.

4.2 A Phased Approach

We offer the following summary of the phased approach. The steps are stated as guidelines PA1 through PA9. They are given in a suggested order of occurrence, recognizing that there are implied feedback loops and iterations and that the exact implications of each step must be determined by the current status of this "bootstrap" process.

PA1: *Make an assessment of current software engineering practices and remedy major shortcomings.*

PA2: *Obtain top-level management support to undertake investigation of reuse feasibility.*

PA3: *Identify one or more application areas (if any) that are important to the organization's mission, are well understood, and have recurring similar software requirements.*

PA4: *Conduct an inventory of reusable assets for the identified application area(s).*

PA5: *Establish an initial library of reusable components.*

PA6: *Determine and conduct a pilot software project employing reuse.*

PA7: *Evaluate experience/success with reuse in the pilot project, present results to management and obtain a decision whether to proceed.*

PA8: *Expand reuse activities to additional application domains and organizational segments, as success and management approval warrant.*

PA9: *Conduct the following activities as part of the practice of software reuse (in the pilot project and in all succeeding reuse efforts):*

(1) *Institute management policies and practices to encourage reuse.*

(2) *Institute/carry out a software engineering process incorporating the creation and use of reusable products.*

(3) *Adjust the organizational structure and staffing as appropriate to support reuse.*

(4) *Implement/update library mechanisms.*

(5) *Perform domain analysis of selected domains and develop/acquire enough reusable components to conduct reuse for the domains.*

(6) *Continually assess the effectiveness of the reuse-based process and adjust/augment it as appropriate.*

4.3 References

Fairley, R., S. L. Pfleeger, T. Bollinger, A. Davis, A. J. Incorvaia, and B. Springsteen. 1989. *Final Report: Incentives for Reuse of Ada Components, vols. 1 through 5.* George Mason University, Fairfax, Va.

Humphrey, W. S., W. L. Sweet, R. K. Edwards, G. R. Lacrois, M. F. Ownes, and H. P. Schultz. September 1987. "A Method for Assessing the Software Engineering Capability of Contractors," CMU/SEI-87-TR-23, Software Engineering Institute, Pittsburgh.

Bibliography

AdaIC (Ada Information Clearinghouse). June 1990. *Ada Information Clearinghouse Newsletter.* 8(2).

Agresti, W., and F. McGarry. March 1988. *The Minnowbrook Workshop on Software Reuse: A Summary Report.* NASA/GSFC, Greenbelt, Md., Computer Sciences Corporation, Beltsville, Md.

Aharonian, G. July 1989. "Working paper." In *Proceedings of the Reuse in Practice Workshop*, ed. J. Baldo and C. Braun. Software Engineering Institute, Pittsburgh, Penn.

Ancoat 1988. *Proceedings of the Sixth National Conference on Ada Technology.* Arlington, Va.

Anderson, C. M., and D. G. McNicholl. 1985. "Reusable Software—A Mission Critical Case Study." In *Proceedings of Compsac 85*, 205.

Arango, G. 1988. *Domain Engineering for Software Reuse.* Ph.D. dissertation, University of California, Irvine, Cal.

Asdjodi, M. 1988. *Knowledge-based Component Composition: An Approach to Software Reusability.* Ph.D. dissertation, The University of Alabama in Huntsville, Huntsville, Ala.

Asdjodi, M., and J. W. Hooper. June 1989. "An Environment for Software Reusability." In *Proceedings of the First International Conference on Software Engineering and Knowledge Engineering*, 48–53. Skokie, Ill.

Bailin, S. C. October 1987. "Informal Rigor: A Practical Approach to Software Reuse." In *Proceedings of the Workshop on Software Reuse*, ed. G. Booch and L. Williams. Rocky Mountain Inst. of Software Engineering, SEI, MCC, Software Productivity Consortium, Boulder, Colo.

Bailin, S. C. May 1989. "An Object-Oriented Requirements Specification Method." *Communications of the ACM* 32(5), 608–23.

Bailin, S. C., and J. M. Moore. December 1987. "A Software Reuse Environment." In *Software Engineering Workshop*. NASA/GSFC, Greenbelt, Md.

Baker, B., and A. Deeds. July 1989. "Industrial Policy and Software Reuse: A Systems Approach." In *Proceedings of the Reuse in Practice Workshop*, ed. J. Baldo and C. Braun. Software Engineering Institute, Pittsburgh, Penn.

Baldo, J., and C. Braun, ed. July 1989. *Proceedings of the Reuse in Practice Workshop*. Software Engineering Institute, Pittsburgh, Penn.

Barnes, B., T. Durek, J. Gaffney, and A. Pyster. July 1987. "Cost Models for Software Reuse." In *Proceedings of the Tenth Minnowbrook Workshop (1987, Software Reuse)*. Blue Mountain Lake, N.Y.

Barnes, B., T. Durek, J. Gaffney, and A. Pyster. October 1987. "A Framework and Economic Foundation for Software Reuse." In *Proceedings of the Workshop on Software Reuse*, ed. G. Booch and L. Williams. Rocky Mountain Inst. of Software Engineering, SEI, MCC, Software Productivity Consortium, Boulder, Colo.

Barsotti, G., and M. Wilkinson. March 1987. "Reusability–Not an Isolated Goal." In *Proceedings of the Conference on Software Reusability and Maintainability*, A1–A14. The National Institute for Software Quality and Productivity, Inc., Tysons Corner, Va.

Barstow, D. November 1985. "Domain-Specific Automatic Programming." *IEEE Trans. on Software Engr.*, **SE-11**(11), 1321-36.

Basili, V. R., H. D. Rombach, J. Bailey, A. Delis, and F. Farhat. March 1989. "Ada Reuse Metrics." In *Guidelines Document for Ada Reuse and Metrics (Draft)*, ed. P. A. Lesslie, R. O. Chester, and M. F. Theofanos, 11–29. K/DSRD-54, Martin Marietta Energy Systems, Inc., Oak Ridge, Tenn., under contract to U.S. Army, AIRMICS.

Basili, V. R., and H. D. Rombach. December 1988. "Towards a Comprehensive Framework for Reuse: A Reuse-Enabling Software Evolution Environment." UMIACS-TR-88-92, University of Maryland, College Park, Md.

Basili, V. R., H. D. Rombach, J. Bailey, and B. G. Joo. July 1987. "Software Reuse: A Framework." In *Proceedings of the Tenth Minnowbrook Workshop (1987, Software Reuse)*. Blue Mountain Lake, N.Y.

Baxter, I. D. October 1987. "Reusing Design Histories via Transformational Systems." In *Proceedings of the Workshop on Software Reuse*, ed. G. Booch and L. Williams. Rocky Mountain Inst. of Software Engineering, SEI, MCC, Software Productivity Consortium, Boulder, Colo.

Bein, J., P. Drew, and R. King. March 1989. "Object-Oriented Data Base Tools to Support Software Engineering." In *Guidelines Document for Ada Reuse and Metrics (Draft)*, ed. P. A. Lesslie, R. O. Chester, and M. F. Theofanos, 95–110. K/DSRD-54, Martin Marietta Energy Systems, Inc., Oak Ridge, Tenn., under contract to U.S. Army, AIRMICS.

Beaver, E. W. July 1989. "Reuse Experiences/Enhancements." In *Proceedings of the Reuse in Practice Workshop*, ed. J. Baldo and C. Braun. Software Engineering Institute, Pittsburgh, Penn.

Belady, L. A. 1989. "Foreword." In *Software Reusability, Vol. I, Concepts and Models*, ed. T. J. Biggerstaff and A. J. Perlis, vii–viii. ACM Press, Addison-Wesley, Reading, Mass.

Biggerstaff, T. J. October 1987. "Hypermedia as a Tool to Aid Large Scale Reuse." In *Proceedings of the Workshop on Software Reuse*, ed. G. Booch and L. Williams. Rocky Mountain Inst. of Software Engineering, SEI, MCC, Software Productivity Consortium, Boulder, Colo.

Biggerstaff, T. J. July 1989. "Design Recovery for Maintenance and Reuse." *Computer* 22(7), 36–49.

Biggerstaff, T. J., and A. J. Perlis, ed. September 1984. "Special Issue on Software Reusability." *IEEE Trans. on Software Engr* SE10(5).

Biggerstaff, T. J., and A. J. Perlis, ed. 1989. *Software Reusability. Concepts and Models*, vol. I, ACM Press, Addison-Wesley, Reading, Mass.

Biggerstaff, T. J., and A. J. Perlis, ed. 1989. *Software Reusability. Applications and Experience*, vol. II, ACM Press, Addison-Wesley, Reading, Mass.

Biggerstaff, T. J., and C. Richter. March 1987. "Reusability Framework, Assessment, and Directions." *IEEE Software* 4(2), 41–49.

Boehm, B. W. 1981. *Software Engineering Economics*. Prentice-Hall, Englewood Cliffs, NJ.

Boehm, B. W. May 1988. "A Spiral Model of Software Development and Enhancement." *Computer* 21(5), 61–72.

Bollinger, T. B. and S. L. Pfleeger. March 1990. "The Economics of Reuse: Issues and Alternatives." In *Proceedings of the Eighth Annual National Conference on Ada Technology*, 436–47. Atlanta, GA.

Booch, G. 1987. *Software Components with Ada.* Benjamin/Cummings, Menlo Park, Calif.

Booch, G. 1987. *Software Engineering With Ada*, 2nd ed. Benjamin/Cummings, Menlo Park, Calif.

Booch, G., and L. Williams, ed. October 1987. *Proceedings of the Workshop on Software Reuse.* Rocky Mountain Inst. of Software Engineering, SEI, MCC, Software Productivity Consortium, Boulder, Colo.

Bott, M. F., and P. J. L. Wallis. 1988. "Ada and Software Re-use." *Software Engineering Journal* 3(5), 177–83.

Braun, C. L., J. B. Goodenough, and R. S. Eaves. April 1985. *Ada Reusability Guidelines.* U.S. Air Force ESD 3285-2-208/2.1, SofTech.

Brooks, F. P. 1987. "No Silver Bullet: Essence and Accidents of Software Engineering." *IEEE Computer* 20(4), 10–19.

Bullard, C. K., D. S. Guindi, W. B. Ligon, W. M. McCracken, and S. Rugaber. March 1989. "Verification and Validation of Reusable Ada Components." In *Guidelines Document for Ada Reuse and Metrics (Draft)*, ed. P. A. Lesslie, R. O. Chester, and M. F. Theofanos, 31–53. K/DSRD-54, Martin Marietta Energy Systems, Inc., Oak Ridge, Tenn., under contract to U.S. Army, AIRMICS.

Burton, B. A., R. W. Aragon, S. A. Bailey, K. D. Koehler, and L. A. Mayes. July 1987. "The Reusable Software Library." *IEEE Software* 4(4), 25–33.

CAMP. 1987. "CAMP, Common Ada Missile Packages, Final Technical Report, Vols. 1, 2, and 3." AD-B-102654,-5,-6. Air Force Armament Laboratory, AFATL/FXG, Eglin AFB, Fla.

Carstensen, H. B., Jr. March 1987. "A Real Example of Reusing Ada Software." In *Proceedings of the Conference on Software Reusability and Maintainability.* The National Institute for Software Quality and Productivity, Inc., Tysons Corner, Va.

Cavaliere, M. J. 1983. "Reusable Code at the Hartford Insurance Group." In *Proceedings of the Workshop on Reusability in Programming.* Newport, R.I.

Cavaliere, M. J. 1989. "Reusable Code at the Hartford Insurance Group" In *Software Reusability. Applications and Experience*, vol. II, ACM Press, Addison-Wesley, Reading, Mass.

Cheatham, T. E. September 1984. "Reusability through Program Transformations." *IEEE Trans. on Software Engr* SE10(5), 589–594.

Chen, Y. F., and C. V. Ramamoorthy. October 1986. "The C Information Abstractor." In *Session of Compsac 86*. Chicago.

Choi, B., R. A. DeMillo, W. Du, and R. Stansifer. March 1989. "Guidelines for Reusing Operational History of Ada Software Components." In *Guidelines Document for Ada Reuse and Metrics (Draft)*, ed. P. A. Lesslie, R. O. Chester, and M. F. Theofanos, 55–66. K/DSRD-54, Martin Marietta Energy Systems, Inc., Oak Ridge, Tenn., under contract to U.S. Army, AIRMICS.

Cleaveland, J. July 1988. "Building Application Generators." *IEEE Software* 5(6), 25–33.

Cohen, J. July 1989. "GTE Software Reuse for Information Management Systems." In *Proceedings of the Reuse in Practice Workshop*, ed. J. Baldo and C. Braun. Software Engineering Institute, Pittsburgh, Penn.

Conn, R. February 1986. "Overview of the DoD Ada Software Repository." *Dr. Dobb's Journal*, 60–61, 86–93.

Curtis, B. 1989. "Cognitive Issues in Reusing Software Artifacts." In *Software Reusability. Applications and Experience*, vol. II, Biggerstaff, T. J., and A. J. Perlis, 269-87. ACM Press, Addison-Wesley, Reading, Mass.

Davis, A. October 1986. "Reusability of Program Code." In *Proceedings of Compsac 86*. Chicago.

DeMillo, R. A., W. Du, and R. Stansifer. June 1989. "Reuse Oriented Ada Programming–A Prototype System," In *Proceedings of the Ada Reuse and Metrics Workshop*. Atlanta.

Deutsch, L. P. 1989. "Design Reuse and Frameworks in the Smalltalk-80 System." In *Software Reusability. Applications and Experience*, vol. II, Biggerstaff, T. J., and A. J. Perlis, 57–71. ACM Press, Addison- Wesley, Reading, Mass.

Druffel, L., and B. Meyer, ed. April 1988. *Proceedings of the 10th International Conference on Software Engineering*. Singapore.

Dusink, E. M. July 1989. "Towards a Design Philosophy for Reuse." In *Proceedings of the Reuse in Practice Workshop*, ed. J. Baldo and C. Braun. Software Engineering Institute, Pittsburgh, Penn.

EVB Software Engineering, Inc. March 1987. "Creating Reusable Ada Software." In *Proceedings of the Conference on Software Reusability and Maintainability*, E1–E58.

Fairley, R., S. L. Pfleeger, T. Bollinger, A. Davis, A. J. Incorvaia, and B. Springsteen. 1989. *Final Report: Incentives for Reuse of Ada Components, vols. 1 through 5*. George Mason University, Fairfax, Va.

Finkelstein, A. 1988. "Reuse of Formatted Requirements Specifications." *Software Engineering Journal* 3(5), 186–97.

Fischer, G. July 1987. "Cognitive View of Reuse and Redesign." *IEEE Software* 4(4), 60–72.

Frakes, W. B., and B. A. Nejmeh. January 1987. "Software Reuse through Information Retrieval." In *Proceedings of the Twentieth Hawaii International Conference on System Sciences*, ed. B. D. Shriver and R. H. Sprague, Jr., 530–35. Kailua-Kona, Hawaii.

Freeman, P. 1987. *Tutorial: Software Reusability*. IEEE Computer Society.

Fujino, K. October 1987. "Software Factory Engineering: Today and Future." In *Proceedings of The 1987 Fall Joint Computer Conference*, 262–70. Dallas.

Gagliano, R. A., M. D. Fraser, and G. S. Owen. March 1989. "Guidelines for Reusable Ada Library Tools." In *Guidelines Document for Ada Reuse and Metrics (Draft)*, ed. P. A. Lesslie, R. O. Chester, and M. F. Theofanos, 79–90. K/DSRD-54, Martin Marietta Energy Systems, Inc., Oak Ridge, Tenn., under contract to U.S. Army, AIRMICS.

Gautier, B. 1988. "Book Review: Software Components with Ada (by Grady Booch)." *Software Engineering Journal* 3(5), 184–85.

Gautier, R. J. and P. J. L. Wallis. 1990. *Software Reuse with Ada*. Peter Peregrinus Ltd., London, U.K.

Geary, K. 1988. "The Practicalities of Introducing Large-Scale Software Re-use." *Software Engineering Journal* 3(5), 172–76.

Goel, A. L., and F. McGarry. July 1987. *Proceedings of the Tenth Minnowbrook Workshop on Software Reuse*, Blue Mountain Lake, NY.

Goguen, J. A. February 1986. "Reusing and Interconnecting Software Components." *IEEE Computer* **19**(2), 16–28.

Grabow, P. C. October 1985. "Software Reuse: Where Are We Going?" In *Proceedings of Compsac 85*, 202. Chicago.

Green, C. R. November 1989. *Proceedings of the Strategic Defense System Software Reuse Workshop*, U.S. Army Strategic Defense Command, Huntsville, Ala.

Guerrieri, E. March 1988. "Searching for Reusable Software Components with the Rapid Center Library System." In *Proceedings of the Sixth National Conference on Ada Technology*, 395–406. Arlington, Va.

Hall, P. A. V. January 1987. "Software Components and Reuse–Getting More Out of Your Code." *Information and Software Technology* **29**(1), 38–43.

Hall, P. A. V. December 1987. "Software Components and Reuse." *Computer Bulletin*, 14–15, 20.

Hall, P. A. V. 1988. "Software Components and Reuse." a special section in *Software Engineering Journal* **3**(5), 171.

Hartman, D. February 1989. "Rapid Prototyping Using Reuse." In *Reuse and the Software Revolution Symposium*. Falcon Air Force Base, Colo.

Hess, J. A., W. E. Novak, P. C. Carroll, S. G. Cohen, R. R. Holibaugh, K. C. Kang, and A. S. Peterson. June 1990. "A Domain Analysis Bibliography." CMU/SEI-90-SR-3.

Hocking, D. E. March 1988. "The Next Level of Reuse." In *Ancoat 1988 Proceedings of the Sixth National Conference on Ada Technology*, 107–10. Arlington, Va.

Holibaugh, R. October 1987. "Overcoming Some Impediments to Software Reuse." In *Proceedings of the Workshop on Software Reuse*, ed. G. Booch and L. Williams. Rocky Mountain Inst. of Software Engineering, SEI, MCC, Software Productivity Consortium, Boulder, Colo.

Holibaugh, R. July 1989. "Reuse: Where to Begin and Why?" In *Proceedings of the Reuse in Practice Workshop*, ed. J. Baldo and C. Braun. Software Engineering Institute, Pittsburgh, Penn.

Hooper, J. W. July 1988. "Simulation Model Reuse: Issues and Approaches." In *Proceedings of The 1988 Summer Computer Simulation Conference*, 51–56. Seattle.

Hooper, J. W. April 1989. *A Perspective of Software Reuse.* ASQBG-I-89-025, U.S. Army AIRMICS.

Hooper, J.W. and R.O. Chester. April 1990. *Software Reuse Guidelines.* U.S. Army AIRMICS ASQB-GI-90-015.

Horowitz, E., and J. B. Munson. September 1984. "An Expansive View of Reusable Software." *IEEE Trans. on Software Engr* **SE10**(5), 477–87.

Huang, C. 1985. "Reusable Software Implementation Technology: A Review of Current Practices." In *Proceedings of Compsac 85*, 207.

Humphrey, W. S. June 1989. "The Software Engineering Process: Definition and Scope." *Software Engineering Notes* 14(4), 82–83.

Humphrey, W. S., W. L. Sweet, R. K. Edwards, G. R. Lacrois, M. F. Ownes, and H. P. Schultz. September 1987. "A Method for Assessing the Software Engineering Capability of Contractors," CMU/SEI-87-TR-23, Software Engineering Institute, Pittsburgh.

Hutchinson, J. W., and P. G. Hindley. 1988. "A Preliminary Study of Large-Scale Software Reuse." *Software Engineering Journal* **3**(5), 208–12.

Iscoe, N. October 1987. "A Knowledge Based and Object-Oriented Approach to Reusability Within Application Domains." In *Proceedings of the Workshop on Software Reuse*, ed. G. Booch and L. Williams. Rocky Mountain Inst. of Software Engineering, SEI, MCC, Software Productivity Consortium, Boulder, Colo.

ISEC (U.S. Army Information Systems Engineering Command). December 1985. *ISEC Reusability Guidelines.* U.S. Army Information Systems Engineering Command 3285-4-247/2, Softech Inc., Waltham, Mass.

Jette, C., and R. Smith. 1989. "Examples of Reusability in an Object-Oriented Programming Environment." In *Software Reusability, Vol. II, Concepts and Models*, ed. T. J. Biggerstaff and A. J. Perlis, 73–101. ACM Press, Addison-Wesley, Reading, Mass.

Joiner, H. F. July 1989. "Position Paper on Software Reuse." In *Proceedings of the Reuse in Practice Workshop*, ed. J. Baldo and C. Braun. Software Engineering Institute, Pittsburgh, Penn.

Jones, G. October 1987. "Methodology/Environment Support for Reusability." In *Proceedings of the Workshop on Software Reuse*, ed. G. Booch and L. Williams. Rocky Mountain Inst. of Software Engineering, SEI, MCC, Software Productivity Consortium, Boulder, Colo.

Jones, T. C. September 1984. "Reusability in Programming: A Survey of the State of the Art." *IEEE Trans. on Software Engr* **SE10**(5), 488–94.

Jones, A., R. E. Bozeman, and W. McIver. March 1989. "A Framework for Library and Configuration Management." In *Guidelines Document for Ada Reuse and Metrics (Draft)*, ed. P. A. Lesslie, R. O. Chester, and M. F. Theofanos, 63–78. K/DSRD-54, Martin Marietta Energy Systems, Inc., Oak Ridge, Tenn., under contract to U.S. Army, AIRMICS.

Kaiser, G. E., and D. Garlan. July 1987. "Melding Software Systems from Reusable Building Blocks." *IEEE Software* **4**(4), 17–24.

Kang, K. C. October 1987. "A Reuse-Based Software Development Methodology." In *Proceedings of the Workshop on Software Reuse*, ed. G. Booch and L. Williams. Rocky Mountain Inst. of Software Engineering, SEI, MCC, Software Productivity Consortium, Boulder, Colo.

Kang, K. C. July 1989. "Features Analysis: An Approach to Domain Analysis." In *Proceedings of the Reuse in Practice Workshop*, ed. J. Baldo and C. Braun. Software Engineering Institute, Pittsburgh, Penn.

King, R. March 1989. "Object-Oriented Data Base Modeling and Software Environments." In *Guidelines Document for Ada Reuse and Metrics (Draft)*, ed. P. A. Lesslie, R. O. Chester, and M. F. Theofanos, 91–94. K/DSRD-54, Martin Marietta Energy Systems, Inc., Oak Ridge, Tenn., under contract to U.S. Army, AIRMICS.

Kitaoka, B. J. July 1989. "Managing Large Repositories for Reuse." In *Proceedings of the Reuse in Practice Workshop*, ed. J. Baldo and C. Braun. Software Engineering Institute, Pittsburgh, Penn.

Lanergan, R. G., and C. A. Grasso. September 1984. "Software Engineering with Reusable Design and Code." *IEEE Trans. on Software Engr* **SE10**(5), 498–501.

Lee, K. J., and M. Rissman. July 1989. "Application of Domain-Specific Software Architectures to Aircraft Flight Simulators and Training Devices." In *Proceedings of the Reuse in Practice Workshop*, ed. J. Baldo and C. Braun. Software Engineering Institute, Pittsburgh, Penn.

Lesslie, P. A., R. O. Chester, and M. F. Theofanos, ed. March 1989. *Guidelines Document for Ada Reuse and Metrics (Draft)*. K/DSRD-54, Martin

Marietta Energy Systems, Inc., Oak Ridge, Tenn., under contract to U.S. Army, AIRMICS.

Lieberherr, K. J., and A. J. Riel. April 1988. "Demeter: A Case Study of Software Growth through Parameterized Classes." In *Proceedings of the 10th International Conference on Software Engineering*, 254–64. Singapore.

Lubars, M. D. October 1987. "Wide-Spectrum Support for Software Reusability." In *Proceedings of the Workshop on Software Reuse*, ed. G. Booch and L. Williams. Rocky Mountain Inst. of Software Engineering, SEI, MCC, Software Productivity Consortium, Boulder, Colo.

Lubars, M. D. and M. T. Harandi. 1989. "Addressing Software Reuse Through Knowledge-Based Design." In *Software Reusability, Vol. II, Concepts and Models*, ed. T. J. Biggerstaff and A. J. Perlis, 345–77. ACM Press, Addison- Wesley, Reading, Mass.

Machida, S. 1985. "Approaches to Software Reusability in Telecommunications Software System." In *Proceedings of Compsac 85*, 206.

Martin, J. 1985. *Fourth Generation Languages, Vol I, Principles.* Prentice-Hall, Englewood Cliffs, N.J.

Matsumoto, Y. 1989. "Some Experiences in Promoting Reusable Software: Presentation in Higher Abstract Levels." In *Software Reusability. Applications and Experience*, vol. II. ACM Press, Addison-Wesley, Reading, Mass.

McCain, R. October 1985. "Reusable Software Component Construction: A Product-Oriented Paradigm." In *Proceedings of the 5th AIAA/ACM/NASA/IEEE Computers in Aerospace Conference*, Long Beach, Cal., 125- -135.

McKay, C. W. March 1989. "Conceptual and Implementation Models." In *Guidelines Document for Ada Reuse and Metrics (Draft)*, ed. P. A. Lesslie, R. O. Chester, and M. F. Theofanos, 111–48. K/DSRD-54, Martin Marietta Energy Systems, Inc., Oak Ridge, Tenn., under contract to U.S. Army, AIRMICS.

McNicholl, D. G., C. Palmer, S. G. Cohen, W. H. Whitford, and G. O. Goeke. 1986. *Common Ada Missile Packages (CAMP), Vol I: Overview and Commonality Study Results.* AFATL-TR-85-93, McDonnell Douglas, St. Louis.

Meyer, B. March 1987. "Reusability: The Case for Object-Oriented Design." *IEEE Software* 4(2), 50–64.

Mittermeir, R. T., and W. Rossak. October 1987. "Software Bases and Software Archives: Alternatives to Support Software Reuse." In *Proceedings of The 1987 Fall Joint Computer Conference*, 21–28. Dallas.

Murine, G. E. March 1987. "Recent Japanese Advances in Reusability and Maintainability." In *Proceedings of the Conference on Software Reusability and Maintainability*, I1–I15. ed. E. Yourdon, The National Institute for Software Quality and Productivity, Inc., Tysons Corner, Va.

Myers, W. July 1990. "'We Want to Write Less Code,' Asserts Symposium Keynoter." *Computer* **23**(7), 117-118.

Neighbors, J. M. 1981. *Software Construction Using Components*. Ph.D. dissertation, University of California, Irvine, Cal.

Neighbors, J. M. September 1984. "The Draco Approach to Constructing Software from Reusable Components." *IEEE Trans. on Software Engr* **SE10**(5), 564–74.

Neighbors, J. M. October 1987. "Report on the Domain Analysis Working Group Session." In *Proceedings of the Workshop on Software Reuse*, ed. G. Booch and L. Williams. Rocky Mountain Inst. of Software Engineering, SEI, MCC, Software Productivity Consortium, Boulder, Colo.

Nissen, J., and P. Wallis. 1984. *Portability and Style in Ada*. Cambridge University Press, Cambridge, Mass.

Notkin, D., and W. G. Griswold. April 1988. "Extension and Software Development." In *Proceedings of the 10th International Conference on Software Engineering*, 274–83. Singapore.

Novak, W. E. June 1990. "U.S. Army SDS CRWG Reuse Committee Technical Requirements Document: Technical Guidance Section." (Preliminary Draft).

Onuegbe, E. O. January 1987. "Software Classification as an Aid to Reuse: Initial Use as Part of a Rapid Prototyping System." In *Proceedings of the Twentieth Hawaii International Conference on System Sciences*, ed. B. D. Shriver and R. H. Sprague, Jr., 521–29. Kailua-Kona, Hawaii.

Oskarsson, O. 1983. "Reusability of Modules with Strictly Local Data and Devices." in *ITT Proceedings of the Workshop on Reusability in Programming*. Newport, R. I.

Oskarsson, O. 1989. "Reusability of Modules with Strictly Local Data and Devices–A Case Study" In *Software Reusability. Applications and Experience*, vol. II, ACM Press, Addison-Wesley, Reading, Mass.

Palmer, C. July 1989. "Reuse in Practice." In *Proceedings of the Reuse in Practice Workshop*, ed. J. Baldo and C. Braun. Software Engineering Institute, Pittsburgh, Penn.

Parnas, D. L. 1972. "On the Criteria to be Used in Decomposing Systems into Modules." *Communications of the ACM* 15(12).

Perry, J. M., and M. Shaw. July 1989. "The Role of Domain Independence in Promoting Software Reuse." In *Proceedings of the Reuse in Practice Workshop*, ed. J. Baldo and C. Braun. Software Engineering Institute, Pittsburgh, Penn.

Plinta, C. July 1989. "A Model Solution for the C^3I Domain." In *Proceedings of the Reuse in Practice Workshop*, ed. J. Baldo and C. Braun. Software Engineering Institute, Pittsburgh, Penn.

Presson, P. E., J. Tsai, T. P. Bowen, J. V. Post, and R. Schmidt. July 1983. *Software Interoperability and Reusability Guidebook for Software Quality Measurement, vols. I and II*. Boeing Aerospace Co.

Prieto-Diaz, R. October 1987. "Domain Analysis for Reusability." In *Proceedings of Compsac 87*, 23–29. Tokyo.

Prieto-Diaz, R. October 1987. "Faceted Classification and Reuse Across Domains." In *Proceedings of the Workshop on Software Reuse*, ed. G. Booch and L. Williams. Rocky Mountain Inst. of Software Engineering, SEI, MCC, Software Productivity Consortium, Boulder, Colo.

Prieto-Diaz, R., April 1990. "Domain Analysis: An introduction." *ACM Software Eng. Notes* 15(2), 47–54.

Prieto-Diaz, R., and P. Freeman. January 1987. "Classifying Software for Reusability." *IEEE Software* 4(1), 6–16.

Prywes, N. S., and E. D. Lock. 1989. "Use of the Model Equational Language and Program Generator by Management Professionals" In *Software Reusability. Applications and Experience*, vol. II, ACM Press, Addison-Wesley, Reading, Mass.

Pyster, A., and B. Barnes. December 1987. *The Software Productivity Consortium Reuse Program*. SPC-TN-87-016, Software Productivity Consortium, Reston, Va.

Ramamoorthy, C. V., V. Garg, and A. Prakash. October 1986. "Support for Reusability in Genesis." In *Proceedings of Compsac 86*, 299–305. Chicago.

Ramamoorthy, C. V., and R. T. Yeh, ed. October 1987. *Proceedings of the 1987 Fall Joint Computer Conference.* Dallas.

Reifer, D.J. June 1990. "Joint Integrated Avionics Working Group Reusable Software Program Operational Concept Document (OCD)" (Draft). RCI- TR-075B, Reifer Consultants, Inc. (Torrance, CA).

Rice, J. G. 1981. *Build Program Technique: A Practical Approach for the development of Automatic Software Generation Systems.* Wiley, New York.

Rogerson, A. M., and S. C. Bailin. July 1987. "Software Reusability Environment Prototype: Experimental Approach." In *Proceedings of The Tenth Minnowbrook Workshop.* Software Reuse, Blue Mountain Lake, N.Y.

St. Dennis, R. J. May 1986. *A Guidebook for Writing Reusable Source Code in Ada (R), Version 1.1.* CSC-86-3:8213, Honeywell, Golden Valley, Minn.

St. Dennis, R. J. January 1987. "Reusable Ada Software Guidelines." In *Proceedings of the Twentieth Hawaii International Conference on System Sciences*, ed. B. D. Shriver and R. H. Sprague, Jr., 513–20. Kailua-Kona, Hawaii.

Sayani, H. March 1987. "Applications In Reverse Software Engineering." In *Proceedings of the Conference on Software Reusability and Maintainability*, ed. E. Yourdon, L1–L15. The National Institute for Software Quality and Productivity, Inc., Tysons Corner, Va.

SEI (Software Engineering Institute). June 1990. "Domain Analysis Project" (Briefing Charts presented by W.E. Novak at SDIO Reuse Committee Meeting, National Test Bed, Falcon AFB (Colorado Springs), CO).

Selby, R. W. 1989. "Quantitative Studies of Software Reuse," In *Software Reusability: Vol. II Applications and Experience*, ed. T. J. Biggerstaff and A. J. Perlis, 213-33.

Shriver, B. D., and R. H. Sprague, Jr., ed. January 1987. *Proceedings of the Twentieth Hawaii International Conference on System Sciences.* Kailua-Kona, Hawaii.

Simos, M. A. October 1987. "The Domain-Oriented Software Life Cycle: Towards an Extended Process Model for Reusability." In *Proceedings of the Workshop on Software Reuse*, ed. G. Booch and L. Williams. Rocky Mountain Inst. of Software Engineering, SEI, MCC, Software Productivity Consortium, Boulder, Colo.

Smith, S. R. 1989. *An Advanced Full-Text Information Retrieval System*. Ph.D. dissertation, The University of Alabama, Huntsville, Ala.

Solderitsch, J. July 1989. "The Reusability Library Framework: Working Toward an Organon." In *Proceedings of the Reuse in Practice Workshop*, ed. J. Baldo and C. Braun. Software Engineering Institute, Pittsburgh, Penn.

Soloway, E., and K. Ehrlich. September 1984. "Empirical Studies of Programming Knowledge." *IEEE Trans. on Software Eng.* **SE-10**(5).

Standish, T. A. September 1984. "An Essay on Software Reuse." *IEEE Trans. on Software Engr.* **SE10**(5), 494–97.

Tarumi, H., K. Agusa, and Y. Ohno. April 1988. "A Programming Environment Supporting Reuse of Object- Oriented Software." In *Proceedings of the 10th International Conference on Software Engineering*, 265–73. Singapore.

Taylor, C. July 1989. "Software Reuse." In *Proceedings of the Reuse in Practice Workshop*, ed. J. Baldo and C. Braun. Software Engineering Institute, Pittsburgh, Penn.

Tracz, W. January 1987. "RECIPE: A Reusable Software Paradigm." In *Proceedings of the Twentieth Hawaii International Conference on System Sciences*, ed. B. D. Shriver and R. H. Sprague, Jr., 546–55. Kailua-Kona, Hawaii.

Tracz, W. July 1987. "Making Reuse a Reality." *IEEE Software* 4(4).

Tracz, W. October 1987. "Software Reuse Myths." In *Proceedings of the Workshop on Software Reuse*, ed. G. Booch and L. Williams. Rocky Mountain Inst. of Software Engineering, SEI, MCC, Software Productivity Consortium, Boulder, Colo.

Tracz, W. 1988. *Tutorial. Software Reuse: Emerging Technology*. IEEE Computer Society.

Tracz, W. 1988. "Ada Reusability Efforts: A Survey of the State of the Practice." In *Tutorial: Software Reuse: Emerging Technology*, 23–32. IEEE Computer Society.

Tracz, W. April 1990. "Where Does Reuse Start?" *ACM Software Eng. Notes* 15(2), 42-46.

Tully, C., ed. June 1989. "Proceedings of the 4th International Software Process Workshop, Devon UK, May, 1988." *Software Engineering Notes* 14(4), 82–83.

Utter, D. F. 1985. "Reusable Software Requirements Documents." *Proceedings of Compsac 85,* 204.

Van Scoy, R., and C. Plinta. July 1989. "An Informal Experiment in Reuse." In *Proceedings of the Reuse in Practice Workshop,* ed. J. Baldo and C. Braun. Software Engineering Institute, Pittsburgh, Penn.

Vogelsong, T. July 1989. "Reusable Ada Packages for Information System Development (RAPID)–An Operational Center of Excellence for Software Reuse." In *Proceedings of the Reuse in Practice Workshop,* ed. J. Baldo and C. Braun. Software Engineering Institute, Pittsburgh, Penn.

Wald, E. 1986. *STARS Reusability Guidebook, V4.0* (Draft). U.S. Department of Defense, STARS.

Wegner, P. July 1984. "Capital-Intensive Software Technology." *IEEE Software* 1(3).

Wong, W. 1986. *A Management Overview of Software Reuse,* 500-142, National Bureau of Standards, Washington, D.C.

Wood, M., and I. Sommerville. 1988. "An Information Retrieval System for Software Components." *Software Engineering Journal* 3(5), 198–207.

Yamamoto, S., and S. Isoda. October 1986. "SOFTDA–A Reuse-Oriented Software Design System " In *Proceedings of Compsac 86,* 284–90. Chicago.

Yeh, R. T., and T. A. Welch. October 1987. "Software Evolution: Forging a Paradigm." In *Proceedings of The 1987 Fall Joint Computer Conference,* 10–12. Dallas.

Yourdon, E., ed. March 1987. *Proceedings of the Conference on Software Reusability and Maintainability.* The National Institute for Software Quality and Productivity, Inc., Tysons Corner, Va.

Zave, P. February 1984. "The Operational Versus the Conventional Approach to Life Cycle Development." *ACM Communications* 27(2).

Appendix A: Collected Guidelines

Contents

The following is a complete listing of the software reuse guidelines presented in this book. An attempt has been made to arrange the guidelines in the logical order for operational implementation. Following each guideline is a page number in square brackets. This is the page in the body of this book that first presents the guideline.

Each guideline has been given a unique identifier, for example PA1, to simplify referring to each guideline. PA1 through PA9 are top level guidelines describing a phased approach to implementation of a reuse program. MS1 through MS13 are the guidelines pertaining to organizational management and structure. OB1 and OB2 relate to organizational behavior. CL1 through CL5 are contractual and legal guidelines. F1 through F4 are financial guidelines. SP1 through SP10 are the software process guidelines. DA1 through DA6 are domain analysis guidelines. CC1 through CC20 are component creation guidelines. Guidelines for reusing components are labeled RC1 through RC13. Quality guidelines are labeled Q1 through Q4. Verification and validation guidelines are labeled V1 through V8. Coding guidelines for Ada code reuse are presented in Appendix B.

Guidelines are introduced in chapters 2, 3, and 4 as the discussion develops the rationale and background for the guidelines. As a result, guidelines in a top level category are not always listed sequentially under one heading. For example, CC15 through CC18 are component creation guidelines that relate to classifying and storing components and are therefore listed in section A.2.1.3, Classifying and Storing Components. We do not feel this detracts from the utility of the guideline identifiers, but enhances their utility by indicating the category of guideline that addresses the section topic.

A.1 Getting Started

PA1: *Make an assessment of current software engineering practices and remedy major shortcomings. [p. 139]*

PA2: *Obtain top-level management support to undertake investigation of reuse feasibility. [p. 139]*

PA3: *Identify one or more application areas (if any) that are important to the organization's mission, are well understood, and have recurring similar software requirements. [p. 139]*

PA4: *Conduct an inventory of reusable assets for the identified application area(s). [p. 139]*

PA5: *Establish an initial library of reusable components. [p. 139]*

PA6: *Determine and conduct a pilot software project employing reuse. [p. 139]*

PA7: *Evaluate experience/success with reuse in the pilot project, present results to management and obtain a decision whether to proceed. [p. 139]*

PA8: *Expand reuse activities to additional application domains and organizational segments, as success and management approval warrant. [p. 139]*

PA9: *Conduct the following activities as part of the practice of software reuse (in the pilot project and in all succeeding reuse efforts):*

  (1) *Institute management policies and practices to encourage reuse.*

  (2) *Institute/carry out a software engineering process incorporating the creation and use of reusable products.*

  (3) *Adjust the organizational structure and staffing as appropriate to support reuse.*

  (4) *Implement/update library mechanisms.*

  (5) *Perform domain analysis of selected domains and develop/acquire enough reusable components to conduct reuse for the domains.*

  (6) *Continually assess the effectiveness of the reuse-based process and adjust/augment it as appropriate. [p. 139]*

A.2 Managerial Guidelines

A.2.1 Managerial Issues

A.2.1.1 Organizational Management and Structure

MS1: *Upper-level management must set reuse goals, create an organizational infrastructure to support software reuse, establish policies, and provide necessary resources. [p. 21]*

MS2: *Mid-level management must develop procedures, populate the organizational structure, allocate resources, and establish controls and metrics to achieve goals. [p. 21]*

MS3: *Project-level management and technical personnel must carry out the reuse/reusability activities in individual projects. [p. 21]*

MS4: *Establish an organizational entity whose charter is to promote reuse considerations at the corporate level. [p. 22]*

MS5: *Evaluate the suitability of establishing the reuse matrix structure and domain reuse groups. [p. 22]*

MS6: *Structure software development by domains amenable to reuse considerations. [p. 22]*

MS7: *Establish strong connections between reuse and maintenance activities. [p. 22]*

MS8: *Provide different types of training for managers, developers, and domain reuse specialists. [p. 22]*

MS9: *Make personnel assignments that take reuse and reusability into account. [p. 22]*

MS10: *Assign reuse facilitators to development groups. [p. 22]*

MS11: *Allow two to three years after initiating software reuse before expecting economic advantages from the program. [p. 22]*

MS12: *Provide a corporate financial "safety net" for projects practicing reuse; provide funding for generation of reusable components. [p. 22]*

MS13: *Managers in federal organizations must take the initiative to influence the adoption of reuse within their own organizations and within contracts they direct. [p. 22]*

MS14: *Be realistic. Do not promise too much, too soon. [p. 22]*

A.2.1.2 Organizational Behavior

OB1: *Provide incentive rewards to participate in reuse. [p. 23]*

OB2: *Seek to enhance psychological job satisfaction to motivate willing participation in reuse. [p. 23]*

A.2.1.3 Contractual and Legal Considerations

CL1: *Seek contractual means to require or to encourage contractors to create reusable software (from which the government gains future benefits) and to reuse existing software (which gives the government immediate benefits). [p. 25]*

CL2: *Establish and enforce reuse practices within government development groups. [p. 26]*

CL3: *Require reuse within a group of related contracts (e.g., by a prime contractor and subcontractors). [p. 26]*

CL4: *Seek means to alter project funding approaches to encourage creation of reusable software. [p. 26]*

CL5: *Seek resolution to the legal issues of potential liability and partial ownership. [p. 26]*

A.2.1.4 Financial Considerations

F1: *Establish mechanisms to accumulate an organizational database of historical financial data relative to software production and maintenance, including reuse activities. [p. 32]*

F2: *Provide cost-modeling tools, to the extent feasible, in concert with organizational data for reuse/reusability decision assessments (including make versus reuse versus buy decisions). [p. 32]*

F3: *Consider/model costs over multiple projects. [p. 32]*

F4: *Establish mechanisms to share the cost of developing reusable components across multiple projects. [p. 32]*

A.2.2 Software Engineering Process Incorporating Reuse

SP1: *Initiate action to establish a software engineering process (including development and maintenance) that includes reuse and reusability as important, integral, natural, and inescapable elements. [p. 43]*

SP2: *Augment DOD-STD-2167A with refinements that specifically support and encourage reusability and reuse (e.g., the five-step generic reuse/reusability model). [p. 43]*

SP3: *Emphasize effective, consistent methods for all aspects of software development and maintenance. [p. 43]*

SP4: *Automate activities within the software process as understanding and experience permit. [p. 43]*

SP5: *During the requirements determination phase, conduct the following activities:*

(1) *Make use of available requirements components as appropriate.*

(2) *Structure requirements to take advantage of available high-level designs.*

(3) *Emphasize preparation of reusable requirements components (from newly developed requirements and modified previously available requirements). [p. 43]*

SP6: *During the high-level-design phase, conduct the following activities:*

(1) *Make use of available requirements components as appropriate.*

(2) *Structure requirements to take advantage of available high-level designs.*

(3) *Emphasize preparation of reusable high-level-design components (from newly developed high-level designs and modified previously available high-level designs). [p. 43]*

SP7: *During the detailed-design phase, conduct the following activities:*

(1) *Make use of available requirements components as appropriate.*

(2) *Structure requirements to take advantage of available high-level designs.*

(3) *Emphasize preparation of reusable detailed-design components (from newly developed detailed designs and modified previously available detailed designs). [p. 44]*

SP8: *During the coding and unit-testing phase, conduct the following activities:*

(1) *Make use of available requirements components as appropriate.*

(2) *Emphasize preparation of reusable code components and test cases (from newly developed code/test cases and modified previously available code/test cases). [p. 44]*

SP9: *During integration testing, conduct the following activities:*

(1) *Make use of available requirements components as appropriate.*

(2) *Emphasize preparation of reusable test plans/cases/results (from newly developed tests and modified, previously available tests). [p. 44]*

SP10: *Recognizing that the maintenance phase contains as subphases the software development phases, apply to maintenance the guidelines provided above for requirements, design, coding, and testing. [p. 44]*

CC9: *Evaluate object-oriented approaches for use in the software process, considering especially the benefits for reusable components. [p. 83]*

A.3 Technical Guidelines (Relative to the Software Life Cycle)

A.3.1 Guidelines Spanning the Life Cycle

A.3.1.1 General Guidelines

CC1: *Provide domain analysis results within the reuse framework—explicitly and/or implicitly. [p. 69]*

CC2: *Make careful assessments, including financial predictions, in deciding whether to develop a reusable component. [p. 69]*

CC3: *Prepare for reuse all more-abstract life-cycle representations of a reusable component (e.g., prepare requirements specification for a high-level design). [p. 69]*

CC4: *Record and supply adaptation suggestions with a reusable component. [p. 69]*

CC5: *Generalize a reusable component to the extent practical during its preparation. [p. 69]*

CC7: *In preparing components for reuse, seek to separate functionality from context, and to factor out commonality. [p. 74]*

A.3.1.2 Component Quality

Q1: *Set standards to be met by all library components. [p. 94]*

Q2: *Emphasize stringent V&V for reusable components, stressing portability and adaptability. [p. 94]*

Q3: *Emphasize enforcement of standards and practices by the quality assurance group; employ a reusability checklist. [p. 94]*

Q4: *Establish and operate an effective configuration management program for the reuse library. [p. 94]*

V1: *State environment compatibility explicitly in the requirements specification. [p. 94]*

V2: *Specify constraints on the use of reusable components as assertions; include assertions within the component specification and (if practical) within the executable code. [p. 94]*

V3: *Construct code for portability and adaptability (rather than attempting to isolate inadequacies by testing). [p. 95]*

V4: *Parameterize specifications that are dependent on the machine environment so that the behavior of the component is expressed relative to a part of the machine environment. [p. 95]*

V5: *Classify reusable components along each of the dimensions of concurrency, space utilization, space reclamation, and iterator availability; make the classification a part of the component specification. [p. 95]*

V6: *Use suggested classification of reuse errors to recognize or to detect errors automatically; remove errors if possible, or adequately document their existence for location and modification when necessary. [p. 95]*

V7: *Employ a comprehensive testing method, consisting of a combination of approaches, to detect reuse errors (including simulation of the execution environment, static analysis, mutation analysis, and constraint-based analysis). [p. 95]*

V8: *Include adequacy criteria that reduce the amount of testing needed and provide a measure of a test suite's effectiveness. [p. 95]*

A.3.1.3 Classifying and Storing Components

CC15: *Determine approach(es) for classifying and storing components, e.g., based on domain analysis. [p. 100]*

CC16: *Represent relationships between a component and its more (and less) abstract representations (as to life-cycle phase). [p. 100]*

CC17: *Represent relationships between a component and others that may collectively solve a given problem (or class of problems). [p. 100]*

CC18: *Represent relationships between components based on generalization/specialization. [p. 100]*

CC19: *Represent relationships between components based on decomposition (e.g., between a system specification and a subsystem specification). [p. 100]*

CC20: *Document each component thoroughly on-line, including user documentation and programming (i.e., maintenance) documentation. [p. 100]*

A.3.1.4 Searching and Retrieving

RC1: *Devise and implement a mechanism for search and retrieval supporting query and browsing modes. [p. 109]*

RC2: *Emphasize user-friendly interface for search and retrieval. [p. 109]*

RC3: *Provide indication of "goodness of fit" of components to a query. [p. 109]*

A.3.1.5 Understanding and Assessing Components

RC4: *Seek to facilitate understandability of reusable components through effective domain analysis, good software development practices, and good classification and storage mechanisms. [p. 111]*

RC5: *Seek approaches/tools to help understand software not specifically prepared for reuse (e.g., reverse engineering). [p. 111]*

RC6: *Use operational history of components in assessing their suitability for reuse. [p. 111]*

RC7: *Obtain feedback from users of components, including number of uses, degree of satisfaction, and errors. [p. 111]*

A.3.1.6 Adapting Components

RC8: *Use higher-abstraction representations in adapting a component (e.g., use design when adapting code). [p. 114]*

RC9: *Emphasize the use of available metrics/tools to assess adaptation effort. [p. 114]*

RC10: *Conduct testing of resulting code components relative to intended application environments. [p. 114]*

A.3.2 Domain Analysis

DA1: *Select domain(s) carefully for analysis, based on the maturity and stability of the organization's activities within each domain and on the planned emphasis the domain is to receive. [p. 62]*

DA2: *Determine and apply a systematic approach to domain analysis, yielding a domain model, a set of domain terminology, and a domain architecture. [p. 63]*

DA3: *Use domain analysis results as a basis for classifying, storing, and retrieving reusable components. [p. 63]*

DA4: *Use domain analysis results as a basis for decisions about the advisability of investing in specific instances of reusable software. [p. 63]*

DA5: *Use domain analysis results to help understand how existing domain-specific reusable software may be applied. [p. 63]*

DA6: *Take advantage of existing system engineering analyses that identify commonality. [p. 63]*

A.3.3 Requirements Determination

CC6: *State as a requirement the reuse of software and/or the creation of reusable software. [p. 69]*

CC8: *Seek to ease the adaptation effort for specifications and designs by utilizing as much as possible such technologies as application generators, transformation systems, parameterization, and knowledge-based approaches. [p. 74]*

SP5: *During the requirements determination phase, conduct the following activities:*

(1) *Make use of available requirements components as appropriate.*

(2) *Structure requirements to take advantage of available high-level designs.*

(3) *Emphasize preparation of reusable requirements components (from newly developed requirements and modified previously available requirements). [p. 43]*

A.3.4 High-Level Design

CC8: *Seek to ease the adaptation effort for specifications and designs by utilizing as much as possible such technologies as application generators, transformation systems, parameterization, and knowledge-based approaches. [p. 74]*

SP6: *During the high-level-design phase, conduct the following activities:*

(1) *Make use of available requirements components as appropriate.*

(2) *Structure requirements to take advantage of available high-level designs.*

(3) *Emphasize preparation of reusable high-level-design components (from newly developed high-level designs and modified previously available high-level designs). [p. 43]*

A.3.5 Detailed Design

SP7: *During the detailed-design phase, conduct the following activities:*

(1) *Make use of available requirements components as appropriate.*

(2) *Structure requirements to take advantage of available high-level designs.*

(3) *Emphasize preparation of reusable detailed-design components (from newly developed detailed designs and modified previously available detailed designs). [p. 44]*

A.3.6 Coding and Unit Testing

SP8: *During the coding and unit-testing phase, conduct the following activities:*

(1) *Make use of available requirements components as appropriate.*

(2) *Emphasize preparation of reusable code components and test cases (from newly developed code/test cases and modified previously available code/test cases). [p. 44]*

CC10: *Supply reusable code in the form of a generator or a transformation system for greater reuse leverage, when practical. [p. 90]*

CC11: *In preparing code blocks, use generics, parameterized procedures, and code templates for greater reuse generality, as appropriate. [p. 90]*

CC12: *Emphasize good programming style in developing reusable code, creating code exhibiting understandability, reliability, and maintainability. [p. 90]*

CC13: *Emphasize Ada and other programming languages that are suitable for reusable code. [p. 90]*

CC14: *Establish a set of organizational guidelines for code development. [p. 90]*

RC11: *Use existing mechanisms for composition to the extent practical (e.g., procedure linking, UNIX pipes, inheritance in object-oriented languages, etc.) [p. 115]*

RC12: *Seek automated approaches to composition as understanding permits. [p. 115]*

A.3.7 Integration Testing

RC13: *Conduct integration testing as composition is achieved. [p. 115]*

SP9: *During integration testing, conduct the following activities:*

(1) *Make use of available requirements components as appropriate.*

(2) *Emphasize preparation of reusable test plans/cases/results (from newly developed tests and modified, previously available tests). [p. 44]*

A.3.8 Maintenance

SP10: *Recognizing that the maintenance phase contains as subphases the software development phases, apply to maintenance the guidelines provided above for requirements, design, coding, and testing. [p. 44]*

Appendix B: Guidelines for Reusable Ada Code

Contents

The following is a listing of coding and unit testing reuse guidelines for Ada code. These guidelines supplement the more general software reuse guidelines collected in Appendix A. Most of these guidelines are from St. Dennis (1986 and 1987). A discussion and additional references are given in section 3.2.3.2.

Each guideline has been given a unique identifier to simplify referring to each guideline. Guidelines for Ada subprograms, packages, visibility, tasks, program structure, generic units, and exceptions are labeled AS1 through AS12, AP1 through AP6, AV1 through AV4, AT1 through AT16, AP1 through AP9, AG1 through AG15, and AE1 through AE4, respectively.

B.1 Subprograms

AS1: *Separate subprogram declarations and bodies for ease of recompilation and modification.*

AS2: *All reusable subprograms except a main program must be written within a library unit package.*

AS3: *Use subprogram declarations to specify interfaces to reusable objects. Use subprogram bodies to implement these interfaces and properties of the objects.*

169

AS4: *Write subprogram interfaces at an appropriate abstract level.*

AS5: *First-level package-nested subprogram declarations should have a standard format including regions for purpose, parameter descriptions and associated documentation.*

AS6: *Secondary unit (subunit) and first-level package body nested subprogram bodies should have a standard format, including regions for revision history, purpose, associated documentation, parameter description, assumptions/resources required, side effects, diagnostics, data declarations, packages, operations, and algorithmic code.*

AS7: *Write subprogram bodies to effectively handle interaction with/effects on their environment.*

AS8: *Write subprogram bodies with one normal exit and a grouped set of abnormal exits via exception handlers.*

AS9: *Write subprogram bodies to pass results back to callers rather than use results to effect their function.*

AS10: *Exploit formal parameter modes to clarify subprogram interface semantics.*

AS11: *Use named parameter associations for calls on subprograms with more than three parameters or in any case for interface clarity.*

AS12: *Minimize subprogram overloading.*

B.2 Packages

AP1: *Write library unit package specifications and bodies in separate files for ease of recompilation and modification.*

AP2: *Use package specifications to specify the interface to object abstractions; use package bodies to encapsulate implementation-specific details of these abstractions not needed by client software.*

AP3: *Packages should implement interfaces to reusable objects at a consistent abstract level.*

AP4: *Library unit package specifications should have a standard format, including various regions for revision history, purpose, associated documentation, diagnostics, packages, data declarations, operations, and private types.*

AP5: *Secondary unit package bodies should have a standard format including regions for revision history, purpose, associated documentation, assumptions/resources required, side effects, diagnostics, packages, data declarations, operations and initialization code.*

AP6: *Use private or limited private types and the private part of package specifications to restrict client software's view of data and operations on that data.*

B.3 Visibility Rules

AV1: *Do not use* USE *context clauses.*

AV2: *Use renaming declarations to resolve name conflicts with the environment.*

AV3: *Use renaming declarations to facilitate modifying reusable software to represent new object abstractions.*

AV4: *Do not hide package standard (i.e., do not use the identifier* STANDARD *as a user-defined name).*

B.4 Tasks

AT1: *Separate task declarations and bodies for ease of recompilation and modification.*

AT2: *Use task declarations to specify interfaces to reusable objects. Use task bodies to implement these interfaces and properties of the objects.*

AT3: *Write task interfaces at an appropriate abstract level.*

AT4: *First-level package-nested task declarations should have a standard format including regions for purpose, entry descriptions, representation clause descriptions, and associated documentation.*

AT5: *Secondary unit (subunit) and first-level package body nested task bodies should have a standard format including regions for revision history, purpose, associated documentation, assumptions/resources required, side effects, diagnostics, packages, data declarations, operations and algorithmic code.*

AT6: *Write task bodies to effectively handle interaction with/effects on their environment.*

AT7: *Write task bodies with one normal exit or termination point and a grouped set of abnormal exits via exception handlers.*

AT8: *Write task body accept statements to pass results back to callers of the task rather than using results to effect task function.*

AT9: *Use task types to define reusable operations on data and task objects to implement particular (distinct) instances of these operations.*

AT10: *Exploit entry formal parameter modes to clarify task interface semantics.*

AT11: *Group all default parameters in entry parameter specifications at the end of the specifications.*

AT12: *Use named parameter associations for calls to task entries with greater than three parameters or in any case for interface clarity.*

AT13: *Minimize entry overloading.*

AT14: *Write all select statements with an else part or include a handler for the PROGRAM_ERROR exception at the end of the enclosing task block.*

AT15: *Minimize use of task priorities or modify priorities accordingly when composing tasks with other tasks for the sake of reuse.*

AT16: *Minimize use of abort statements.*

B.5. Program Structure and Compilation Issues

APS1: *Use library unit package specifications as the encapsulation mechanism for directly reusable software (i.e., data and operations on the data).*

APS2: *Only first level, nested-nonpackage entities in library unit package specifications form the basis for cataloged, directly reusable objects/software.*

APS3: *Use secondary unit package bodies, package specifications containing only data, and subunits corresponding to first-level package body nested stubs as the encapsulation mechanism for indirectly reusable software.*

APS4: *WITH clauses on package specifications should reference only data needed in specifications. WITH clauses can be used freely on package bodies as needed.*

APS5: *Use subunits to achieve modularity and ease of recompilation.*

APS6: *Do not split an abstraction across several packages. Use layers of packages to reflect the abstraction.*

APS7: *Use separate compilation and separate specifications and bodies to achieve modularity and ease of recompilation.*

APS8: *Implement bodies of subprograms declared in a package specification as subunits of the package body.*

APS9: *Minimize use of Pragma Elaborate.*

B.6 Generic Units

AG1: *Use generic program units (i.e., packages and subprograms) to effectively parameterize reusable software parts.*

AG2: *Use generic program units to precisely specify module interfaces/imports and exports.*

AG3: *Use generics to allow specification of multiple instances of reusable software as compared to reuse of one shared instance.*

AG4: *Use base types rather than subtypes to specify the type of a generic formal object or generic formal subprogram parameter or result types.*

AG5: *Library unit and first-level package-nested generic unit declarations should have a standard format, including a region for description of generic parameters as well as standard information required for non-generic subprogram and package declarations.*

AG6: *Separate generic declarations from bodies for ease of recompilation and modification.*

AG7: *Exploit generic formal object parameter modes to clarify interface semantics.*

AG8: *Use generic type definitions to clarify interface semantics and module operation.*

AG9: *Use additional generic parameters as necessary to effect inheritance of desired operators on generic formal types.*

AG10: *Minimize generic formal subprogram parameter overloading and overloading of subprograms in generic packages.*

AG11: *Minimize use of the box (IS <>) notation to specify default generic formal subprograms as parameters.*

AG12: *Use basic operations/attributes associated with generic formal types to provide required generality to generic bodies.*

AG13: *Use named parameter association in actual parameter parts of generic instantiations.*

AG14: *Use default parameters for generic actual parameters whenever possible.*

AG15: *Create particular instantiations of generic units corresponding to common uses of reusable software.*

B.7 Exceptions

AE1: *For each assumption a subroutine depends on to operate correctly, define an exception that is to be raised when the assumption is violated.*

AE2: *For every situation that would raise an exception, define a function that indicates whether the exception would be raised.*

AE3: *Raise an exception if the user can easily fix the problem. Let the user provide a subprogram to fix the problem if raising an exception causes loss of information.*

AE4: *Provide a subprogram to return all available information describing the nature of an exception situation.*

Index